SOTHEBY COURTAULD EXHIBITION

DRAWING IN BOLOGNA

1500 - 1600

Sponsored by Sotheby's

Elizabeth Llewellyn
Cristiana Romalli

UNIVERSITY OF LONDON
COURTAULD INSTITUTE GALLERIES
18th June – 31st August 1992

Lenders to the Exhibition

Her Majesty Queen Elizabeth II, Windsor Castle

The Duke of Devonshire and the Chatsworth Settlement Trustees

University of London, Courtauld Institute Galleries

The Governing Body of Christ Church, Oxford

Jan and Marie-Anne Krugier

The Janos Scholz Collection,
The Pierpont Morgan Library, New York

Stiftung Ratjen

Jacques Petithory

Dian and Andrea Woodner

Jak Katalan

Private Collections

Foreword

We are delighted to present an exhibition of Bolognese sixteenth century drawings, the fourth in our series of master drawings exhibitions, and the seventh in our new Prints and Drawings Exhibition Room. Not only have the organisers of the exhibition, Mrs. Elizabeth Llewellyn and Mrs. Cristiana Romalli selected some sixty sheets of great aesthetic quality, they have also made a contribution to scholarship in the catalogue which accompanies the exhibition.

None of this would have been possible without the willing cooperation of many private owners, and we are most grateful to Her Majesty Queen Elizabeth II for graciously consenting to lend from the Royal Collection; likewise, we are most indebted to His Grace the Duke of Devonshire, to Christ Church, Oxford, and to Rugby School for their loans; to all the other private owners, many of whom wish to remain anonymous, we extend our warmest thanks. We acknowledge, with gratitude, the generous sponsorship of Sotheby's, without which this exhibition would not have taken place, and thank their Chief Executive, Mr. Tim Llewellyn for his support. We are also very grateful to the Museums and Galleries Commission and to the Department of National Heritage for securing a government indemnity, which has greatly assisted us. I would like to express my personal thanks to Elizabeth Llewellyn and Cristiana Romalli for the highly professional way they have prepared this exhibition in the space of less than a year.

Dennis Farr, Director
Courtauld Institute Galleries

To Philip Pouncey

The art of Bologna in the sixteenth century has been increasingly studied by scholars over the past decades, but is still less familiar than the great achievements of the seventeenth century. Because this exhibition is drawn from private collections alone, it does not pretend to be a comprehensive survey of the subject. We hope, however, that the selection of less well-known works will be instructive and will provide some further understanding of the artistic and intellectual developments of the period. We are grateful to all the lenders, who responded with enthusiasm and generosity to our requests; to Dennis Farr and the staff of the Courtauld Galleries for their cooperation in every aspect of the planning and mounting of the exhibition; and to the scholars, colleagues and friends here and abroad who have shared their knowledge with us. We give special thanks to Myril Pouncey for her particularly generous cooperation.

In a year which sees exhibitions at the Louvre, the Uffizi and the Cini Foundation honouring Philip Pouncey, we wish to dedicate this catalogue to him in acknowledgement of our deepest admiration. The standards he set are daunting, but their rigour was tempered by the warmth of his humour and friendship.

Elizabeth Llewellyn
Cristiana Romalli
Sotheby's, May 1992

Prefazione

Agli inizi del Cinquecento i fatti più significativi della cultura figurativa emiliana riguardano anzitutto la città di Parma, dove le personalità del Correggio e del Parmigianino crearono una 'scuola' che ebbe una risonanza non strettamente locale; l'officina parmense, come in tempi recenti é stata chiamata[1] si arricchì inoltre dell'apporto di Michelangelo Anselmi (affreschi nell'Oratorio della Concezione, purtroppo perduti), un artista di origine toscana, il cui stile inconfondibile influì in modo determinante su maestri quali Girolamo Bedoli (che in seguito si accosterà a Giulio Romano, nella decorazione alla Steccata), e in misura minore il Bertoja che avrà il merito, in seguito al suo trasferimento romano (affreschi nell'Oratorio del Gonfalone, e di Caprarola), di innestare la cultura parmense nell'ambiente dominato dagli Zuccari. Altre personalità 'minori', Giorgio Gandini del Grano, la cui attività grafica é conquista recente della critica [2] e, nella seconda metà del secolo, Giambattista Tinti, e fino al conseguente apparire dello Schedoni, già addentro nel nuovo secolo, completano il panorama figurativo della città emiliana; il cui ruolo-guida ebbe ripercussioni notevoli anche sulla formazione di Niccolò dell'Abate e del Primaticcio prima della definitiva partenza per Fontainebleau[3].

Solo alla fine del Cinquecento si può parlare di una scuola autonoma a Bologna: intorno alla metà del secolo infatti gli artisti bolognesi erano proiettati verso le novità provenienti soprattutto da Firenze, e da Roma; nel quarto decennio due artisti toscani, Francesco Salviati e Giorgio Vasari erano impegnati a Bologna, il primo nell'esecuzione di una pala d'altare in Santa Cristina, il secondo nella decorazione del refettorio di San Michele in Bosco. Inoltre nel 1554 tornava da Roma Pellegrino Tibaldi iniziando a lavorare a Palazzo Poggi, e successivamente in San Giacomo Maggiore. Plasticamente definite e arditamente scorciate, le figure del Tibaldi di stampo michelangiolesco, che si sprigionano illusionisticamente sulle pareti di Palazzo Poggi costituirono un preciso punto di riferimento per la giovane generazione di artisti; Annibale Carracci, *in primis*, si ricorderà dell'impianto compositivo tibaldesco per trasferirlo con nuovi intenti nella Galleria di Palazzo Farnese a Roma. Altri due bolognesi, Lorenzo Sabatini e Orazio Samacchini, aiutarono il Vasari nella decorazione di Palazzo Vecchio a Firenze e in Vaticano; la loro produzione pittorica, e grafica, simile allo stile del maestro aretino, e tra loro spesso confusa per la stretta somiglianza[4], denuncia altresì l'influenza toscana in area bolognese. Un ruolo determinante nella Bologna della seconda metà del secolo l'ebbe anche il fiammingo Dionisio Calvaert, non solo per aver diffuso la conoscenza delle incisioni di Dürer e Luca di Leida, ma per l'importanza data al disegno nella sua bottega; i suoi fogli, a gessetto nero e su carta colorata, non passeranno inosservati agli occhi del giovane Guido Reni, che nella bottega del Calvaert e assieme al Domenichino e all'Albani riceverà i primi rudimenti del mestiere. Diversamente Bartolomeo Passerotti, che preferì la penna, molto prossima alla tecnica incisoria, mostrava uno spiccato interesse per la figura umana (ne é testimonianza l'abbondantissima produzione relativa agli studi di anatomia); così Bartolomeo Cesi, anche se in maniera diversa dal Passerotti, condivise l'interesse per lo studio del disegno dal modello: tipici del maestro gli esempi a matita rossa, che rappresentano garzoni avvolti in mantelli o in abiti talari, in cui la figura umana é amorosamente colta dal vero[5]. Con l'avvento dei Carracci, e di Annibale in particolare, il disegno assume una sua funzione autonoma e indispensabile per la pittura; le loro opere sono basate più che altro sull'osservazione diretta del vero, sugli aspetti della vita quotidiana. L'osservazione della realtà fu accompagnata dallo studio dei maestri del primo Cinquecento, che li portò soprattutto a Parma e Venezia (a meditare sul Correggio e il Parmigianino, Veronese e Tintoretto). La loro attività intensissima, una vera Accademia, riunì insieme un gruppo di assistenti per la gran quantità di commissioni; presto il lavoro di bottega assunse una sua ufficialità con un programma ben preciso fondato sul disegno: esercitazioni dal nudo, dall'antico e tratte dai capolavori del passato esistenti a Bologna, proposti agli allievi. Dal gruppo di questi ultimi ecco emergere la prorompente vitalità di Pietro Faccini, irregolare bolognese[6]. Di carattere battagliero, Faccini uscì ben presto dall'Accademia carraccesca, mentre i suoi dipinti riflettono sia il momento degli affreschi di Palazzo Fava, sia l'incondizionato omaggio al Correggio; palese quest'ultimo nei numerosi disegni a gessetto rosso a noi pervenuti. Gran disegnatore, Faccini sperimentò le tecniche grafiche più diverse: oltre al gessetto rosso, la penna e l'acquerello, eliminando la quadrettatura (retaggio cinquecentesco), mostrando nell'uso della biacca attenzioni all'opera del Tintoretto. Elementi tintoretteschi affiorano anche nell'Elemosina di San Rocco (ora a Dresda, Gemäldegalerie), l'ultima opera di un certo impegno prima della partenza di Annibale per Roma, atta a testimoniare il soggiorno veneziano del maestro alla fine dell'ottavo decennio del secolo. Il momento dei disegni a gessetto rosso, di evidente derivazione correggesca ancora presente negli affreschi di Palazzo Fava e Magnani, lascia il passo ad una maniera più 'forte', dai contrasti chiaroscurali più decisi, così dai disegni a penna e inchiostro scaturisce una realtà più 'cruda', feriale. Non fu estraneo all'influenza tintorettesca nemmeno Agostino; i suoi non numerosi disegni a gessetto nero ne sono una prova evidente. Certamente la produzione più nota di Agostino é quella realizzata con una tecnica (la penna e l'inchiostro) da incisore, che richiama non c'é dubbio quanto già sperimentato dal Passerotti. Anche Ludovico, dei tre Carracci il più ancorato alla sua terra, si dedicava al disegno dal nudo; ma i risultati più felici comprendono gli studi (a penna, inchiostro e acquerello) basati sullo stile grafico del Parmigianino. Partito Agostino per Roma nel 1597, Ludovico assunse la direzione dell'Accademia: e la nuova tendenza, intenta al recupero formalistico della tradizione emiliana, é già manifesta nell'opera di Lucio Massari e Francesco Brizio in San Michele in Bosco. La lezione di Ludovico non fu senza conseguenze per il giovane Reni, e, il Guercino, che fu attratto dagli esempi grafici del Faccini (soprattutto nei ben noti studi di nudo); la strada al Cavedone era già aperta.

Mario di Giampaolo

Footnotes

1: A. Ghidiglia Quintavalle, 'L'Oratorio della Concezione a Parma', *Paragone,* ix, 1958, no.103.

2: K. Oberhuber, review of A.E. Popham, *Drawings by Artists Working in Parma in the Sixteenth Century, Master Drawings,* vol.viii, no.3 (1970).

3. S. Béguin, 'Contribuito allo studio dei disegni del Primaticcio', *Bolletino d'Arte,* vol.xv, 1982.

4. C.C. Malvasia, *Felsina Pittrice: Vite dei Pittori,* 1678, ed. G. Zanotti, Bologna 1841.

5. A. Forlani Tempesti, 'Trentotto disegni del Cesi, comprati da Leopoldo de'Medici', in *Scritti di Storia dell'Arte in Onore di Ugo Procacci,* Venice 1977.

6. F. Arcangeli in *Maestri della Pittura del Seicento Emiliano,* exhib. cat., Bologna 1950.

Introduction

At the beginning of the sixteenth century, the most significant developments in Emilian painting took place in Parma, where Correggio and Parmigianino created a style whose influence spread beyond their city. The Parmese school, *officina parmense* as it has recently been termed by Ghidiglia Quintavalle[1], was also enriched by the contributions of Michelangelo Anselmi who painted frescoes in the Oratorio della Concezione, which are now destroyed. He was an artist of Tuscan origins whose unmistakable style strongly influenced masters such as Girolamo Mazzola Bedoli, who later, in his decorations at the Steccata, drew closer to Giulio Romano, and Jacopo Bertoja, who with his frescoes in the Oratorio del Gonfalone in Rome and at Caprarola, brought Parmese culture into the artistic milieu dominated by Taddeo and Federico Zuccaro. Other "minor" personalities such as Giorgio Gandini del Grano, whose graphic activity has only recently been defined by Oberhuber[2], and Giambattista Tinti, in the second half of the century, and finally Schedone, in the new century, complete the artistic panorama of the Emilian city whose leading rôle had important effects on the formation of Nicolò dell'Abate and of Primaticcio before their departure for Fontainebleau[3].

Only at the end of the sixteenth century can one speak of an independent Bolognese school; in the middle of the century, Bolognese artists were attracted to the new styles emanating above all from Florence and from Rome. In the fourth decade of the century, two Tuscan artists, Francesco Salviati and Giorgio Vasari, were employed in Bologna, the former in painting an altarpiece for Sta. Cristina, the latter in decorating the refectory of S. Michele in Bosco. Then, around 1554, Pellegrino Tibaldi returned from Rome and began work in the Palazzo Poggi and in S. Giacomo Maggiore. Sculpturally defined and dramatically foreshortened, Tibaldi's figures bear the strong stamp of Michelangelo, and, bursting illusionistically from the walls of the Palazzo Poggi, provided a specific point of reference for the young generation of artists. Annibale Carracci was the first to draw upon Tibaldi's compositional scheme and he used it to new effect in the Palazzo Farnese, Rome. Two other Bolognese artists, Lorenzo Sabatini and Orazio Samacchini, assisted Vasari in the decoration of the Palazzo Vecchio in Florence and of the Vatican in Rome. The style of their paintings and drawings is similar to Vasari's, and provides a further example of Tuscan influence on Bolognese art. Malvasia[4] noted that the strong resemblance between the two artists' work often led to a confusion in attributions.

The Flemish artist, Dionys Calvaert, played a dominant role in Bologna in the second half of the century not only because he brought knowledge of the prints of Dürer and Lucas van Leyden, but also because he placed great emphasis on drawing in his workshop. His studies, often in black chalk on blue paper, did not pass unobserved by the young Guido Reni who received his early training in Calvaert's studio together with Domenichino and Albani. Bartolomeo Passerotti, who preferred to draw with a pen in a technique close to an engraver's, showed a lively interest in the human figure as is demonstrated by his very abundant production of anatomical studies. Bartolomeo Cesi shared the same interest in drawing from the studio model, but in a different way from Passerotti. Typical of Cesi are red chalk studies of young men in cloaks or in monastic habits, in which the human form is lovingly transcribed from reality[5]. With the advent of the Carracci, and of Annibale in particular, drawing assumed an autonomous and indispensable function in relation to painting. The works of the Carracci are based more than anything on direct observation of reality and of aspects of daily life. This observation was accompanied by study of the works of the masters of the early sixteenth century, primarily in Parma and Venice: Correggio, Parmigianino, Veronese and Tintoretto. The intense activity of the Carracci brought together a real academy of assistants who were necessary for the completion of the large number of commissions they received. Soon their workshop developed a formal programme based on draughtsmanship: drawings were made after nude models, after the antique and after other masterpieces of the past in Bologna. From this group of students emerged the disruptively energetic Pietro Faccini, a Bolognese eccentric [6]. Of a quarrelsome character, Faccini left the academy quickly, but his paintings reflect the style of the Carraccis' Palazzo Fava frescoes as well as offering the unconditional homage to Correggio which is particularly apparent in his many red chalk drawings. A great draughtsman, Faccini experimented with the most diverse techniques, often eliminating squaring, a sixteenth century tradition, and showing, in his use of white heightening, his knowledge of the work of Tintoretto.

Tintorettesque elements also appear in Annibale Carracci's *Charity of St. Roch* now in the Gemäldegalerie, Dresden, his last important work before his departure for Rome and evidence of his visit to Venice in the late 1580s. The Correggesque style of his red chalk drawings related to the frescoes of the Palazzo Fava and the Palazzo Magnani gives way to a more forceful manner, with more decisive contrasts of *chiaroscuro,* and, in the pen and ink drawings, to a more crude, everyday reality.

Even Agostino was not immune to the influence of Tintoretto - his rare black chalk drawings are a proof of this. His most notable drawings, however, are those realized in an engraver's technique, pen and ink, which clearly recall the style already experimented with by Passerotti. Lodovico, of the three Carracci the most rooted in Bologna, also drew from the nude model, but his best drawings, in pen and ink and wash, are based on the graphic style of Parmigianino. When Agostino left for Rome in 1597, Lodovico assumed the directorship of the Academy and the new trend of Bolognese art, based on a return to the formal Emilian traditions, was soon manifest in the works of artists such as Lucio Massari and Francesco Brizio in S. Michele in Bosco. The example of Lodovico was important for the young Reni and for Guercino, who was himself influenced by the drawings of Faccini, above all his nude studies. From Guercino, the way is opened for Cavedone.

Mario di Giampaolo

Abbreviations

Malvasia, 1969:

C.C. Malvasia, *Le pitture di Bologna,* 1686, ed. A. Emiliani, Bologna 1969.

Fortunati, 1986:

Vera Fortunati Pietrantonio, *Pittura bolognese del '500,* Bologna 1986.

Index

1 **NICOLO DELL'ABATE**
Modena circa 1512 - Fontainebleau? 1571

HERCULES KILLING THE NEMAEAN LION.

Inscribed on the *verso: Leo Neumensius ab Hercule* .... Pen and brown ink and wash heightened with white. Corners made up.
229 by 165mm.

Provenance: Anonymous sale, New York, Sotheby's, 8 January 1991, lot 145

This is a preparatory study for one of Nicolò dell'Abate's frescoes, painted *circa* 1550, in the Sala dei Concerti in the Palazzo Poggi, Bologna (fig.27). It differs from the final composition in its upright format and in the surrounding framing. The decoration of the room combines scenes of contemporary social life with several of the labours of Hercules. Sylvie Béguin has suggested that the iconography was devised by Giovanni Poggi, who became a cardinal in 1551, to contrast the heroic struggle against vice with the more human enjoyment of earthly diversions (see S. Béguin, *Mostra di Nicolò dell'Abate,* Bologna 1969, p.75). Two other drawings related to the *Labours of Hercules* are known: *Hercules and Cerberus,* also a vertical composition but without the drawn frame, in the Hessisches Landesmuseum, Darmstadt and *Hercules killing Geryon,* at Christ Church, Oxford (see Wanda Bergamini, in Fortunati, 1986, vol.i, p.290, one illus. p.327).

Private Collection

2 NICOLO DELL'ABATE
Modena circa 1512 - Fontainebleau? 1571

STUDY OF TWO PUTTI.

Red chalk.
210 by 135mm.

Provenance: N.A. Flinck (L.959); William, 2nd Duke of Devonshire (L.718).

Literature: S. Béguin, 'Dessins inédits de la période italienne de Niccolò dell'Abbate', *Raccolta di saggi dedicati a Roberto Longhi in occasione del suo sessantesimo compleanno,* in *Arte antica e moderna,* xiii-xvi, 1961, p.229, fig.100b; M. di Giampaolo and S. Béguin, *Maestri Emiliani del Secondo Cinquecento,* Florence 1979, p.25; W. Bergamini, 'Nicolò dell'Abate', in Fortunati, 1986, p.292, illus. p.338.

Exhibited: Bologna, Palazzo dell'Archiginnasio, *Mostra di Nicolò dell'Abate,* 1969, p.105, no.47, illus.

This drawing was traditionally attributed to Primaticcio until Sylvie Béguin correctly identified it as a preparatory study for one of the groups of putti dividing the various scenes from the *Life of Camilla* which Nicolò painted in a room in the Palazzo Poggi. The life of the heroic princess of the Volsci is taken from Virgil's *Aeneid.* It is an unusual subject, but Camilla serves as a model of female virtue (see A. Ottani Cavina, *Palazzo Poggi,* Bologna 1988, pp.101-107). Another study of a winged putto at Chatsworth was catalogued by Popham to Parmigianino (see A.E. Popham, *Catalogue of the Drawings of Parmigianino,* New Haven 1971, vol.i, no.731, vol.ii, pl.89) but recently published by Godi as the work of Nicolò dell'Abate, also related to this room (see G. Godi, *Nicolò dell'Abate e la presunta attività del Parmigianino a Soragna,* Parma 1976, p.68, note 86).

The Duke of Devonshire and the Chatsworth Settlement Trustees

3 NICOLO DELL'ABATE
Modena circa 1512 - Fontainebleau? 1571

JUPITER AND SEMELE.

Bears inscription: *Giulio Romano.* Pen and brown ink and wash. Squared in black chalk.
303 by 248mm.

Exhibited: London, Armando Neerman, at The National Book League, *Old Master Drawings,* 1975, no.6.

Literature: J. Byam Shaw, *Drawings by Old Masters at Christ Church, Oxford,* Oxford 1986, vol.i, p.235, under cat. no.880; F.M. Aliberti Gaudioso and E. Gaudioso, *Gli affreschi di Paolo III a Castel Sant'Angelo, 1543-1548,* Rome 1981, vol.i, p.196, no.145 (as Domenico Zaga); New York, Metropolitan Museum of Art, *The Woodner Collection: Master Drawings,* 1990, p.98, under no.30 (as *Jupiter and Juno,* and in previous Woodner exhibition catalogues which included his Nicolò dell'Abate *Rape of Ganymede).*

Both John Gere and Philip Pouncey rejected the recent suggestion (Gaudioso, *op.cit.)* that this drawing is by Zaga, and supported the previous attribution to Nicolò dell'Abate. The profile of Semele is reminiscent of Perino del Vaga's facial types, but the penwork, particularly in the treatment of the eagle, is typical of Nicolò. A very beautiful, highly-finished drawing of the same subject by Nicolò is in the British Museum (inv. no.1895-9-15-678, see J.C. Robinson, *Descriptive Catalogue of the Drawings by the Old Masters, forming the Collection of John Malcolm of Poltalloch, Esq.,* London 1869, no.226). Three others, also of the loves of Jupiter, are in the Albertina as Attributed to Nicolò (nos.514-16).

Private Collection

4 DIONYS CALVAERT
Antwerp circa 1540 - Bologna 1619

ST. GREGORY AND THE MIRACLE OF THE BRANDEUM.

Bears attribution on the backing: *Federico Zuccaro.* Pen and brown ink and wash heightened with white over black chalk.
284 by 265mm.

Provenance: Joseph Klein, New York, his sale and others, London, Sotheby's, 10 October 1974, lot 57 (as P. Fontana); bears two unidentified collector's marks, one on the *recto* and the other on the backing.

Julien Stock identified this is a preparatory study, with differences, for one of Calvaert's most celebrated and admired works, his altarpiece in San Gregorio, Bologna for which he signed the contract in 1581 (fig.15; see Malvasia, 1969, p.113/20-25).

The event depicted comes from the Golden Legend. St. Gregory was asked by the Emperor for a holy relic, but the saint was unwilling to disturb the relic and offered instead the consecrated cloth in which it had been wrapped. The Emperor scorned the gift and returned it, whereupon St. Gregory pierced it with a knife and it bled. This miracle was taken as a demonstration that it is the power of faith which sanctifies a relic.

Private Collection

5 DIONYS CALVAERT
Antwerp circa 1540 - Bologna 1619

THE LAMENTATION OVER THE BODY OF CHRIST.

Pen and brown ink and wash over black chalk heightened with white.
420 by 287mm.

Provenance: Luigi Grassi (bears his collector's mark, not recorded in Lugt).

Exhibited: Milan, Stanza del Borgo, *Antichi Disegni dal xvi al xix Secolo,* 1989, p.18, illus.

This is a preparatory study with differences for Calvaert's painting now in the Galleria Nazionale, Parma (inv. no.387; fig.14). The painting was formerly listed as by Camillo Procaccini but was attributed to Calvaert by A. Ghidiglia-Quintavalle (see *Tesori nascosti della Galleria di Parma,* Parma 1968, p.72, no.104, fig.56). Mario di Giampaolo has published a drawing signed: *Dionisio Fiamengo,* which shows another stage in the evolution of the same composition (see Paris, Grand Palais, *Dessins Anciens,* Piero Scarpa, Venice 1978, no.25, illus.). Stylistically the present drawing can be dated around 1580 and it resembles the *Miracle of St. Gregory* which is of the same period (see cat. no.4).

Private Collection

6 **DIONYS CALVAERT**
Antwerp circa 1540 - Bologna 1619

THE MARRIAGE AT CANA.

Signed and dated: *Dionisio Cal 1598.* Black chalk heightened with white. With some squaring and perspective lines.
402 by 298mm.

Provenance: Bishop of Winchester (his sale, according to an inscription on the old mount); anonymous sale, Los Angeles, Sotheby's, 6 November 1978, lot 3.

Literature: K. Andrews, '*The Marriage at Cana* - a trio by Denys Calvaert', *The Burlington Magazine,* vol.cxxvii, no.992 (November 1985), p.757, fig.13.

In the issue of *The Burlington Magazine* which honoured Philip Pouncey, Keith Andrews published a drawing by Calvaert representing *The Marriage at Cana,* which had recently been acquired by the National Gallery of Scotland. It and the present drawing are both signed and dated *1598,* and, in spite of differences in size, medium and degree of finish, they show only minor differences in composition. Another version, dated *1591,* is in the British Museum and was engraved, in the opposite direction, by Philippe Thomassin in 1592 (fig.13 and Andrews, *op.cit.,* fig.12). Again, there are minor differences in the composition. As Keith Andrews pointed out, it is unclear why Calvaert should repeat himself twice after an interval of eight years.

Private Collection

7 **DIONYS CALVAERT**
Antwerp circa 1540 - Bologna 1619

A SAINT LOOKING UPWARDS, WITH OUTSTRETCHED ARMS.

Red chalk
350 by 245mm.

Exhibited: London, P.&D. Colnaghi, *Master Drawings,* 22nd June-9th July 1988, no.18.

This is an impressive example of Calvaert's skilful use of red chalk for which he was much admired by his contemporaries (see C.C. Malvasia, *Felsina pittrice, 1678,* ed. M. Brascaglia, Bologna 1971, p.165). The drawing, which shows a debt to Correggio, must have been made from a studio model posed so that Calvaert could study the fall of the drapery and the foreshortening of a figure intended to been seen from below.

Private Collection

8 **DIONYS CALVAERT**
Antwerp circa 1540 - Bologna 1619

THE ADORATION OF THE SHEPHERDS.

Pen and brown ink and wash heightened with white, on paper washed blue.
311 by 259mm.

Provenance: E. Maurice Bloch, his sale, New York, Christie's, 9 January 1991, lot 2 (as Roman School); Yvonne Tan Bunzl.

In its technique this drawing recalls those described by Malvasia: '.... *piccioli pensieri ch'ei disegnava su carta azzura lumeggiata di biacca'* (see C.C. Malvasia, *Felsina pittrice, 1678,* ed. M. Brascaglia, Bologna 1971, p.163). The drawing shows some similarities, particularly in the dramatic use of light, to a painting of the same subject in the Galleria Sabauda, Turin. The latter has been dated around 1600 (see T. Montella in Fortunati, 1986, vol.ii, p.686, illus. p.704).

Private Collection

9 AGOSTINO CARRACCI
Bologna 1557 - Parma 1602

STUDY OF FIGURES FOR A MASSACRE OF THE INNOCENTS.

Pen and brown ink. Top right corner repaired.
268 by 237mm.

Provenance: Professor E. Susini (bears his collector's mark), his sale, Paris, Libert and Castor, 4 June 1982, lot 56 (as School of Bandinelli); anonymous sale, London, Christie's, 6-7 July 1987, lot 35 (as Agostino).

Although this drawing cannot be connected with a known work, the energetic composition and the strong cross-hatching are characteristic of Agostino's pen style which evolves from his work as a printmaker. It is similar to a study of *The Twelve Apostles,* now at Budapest, which Czére dates between 1594/98 (see A. Czére, *Disegni di Artisti Bolognesi nel Museo delle Belle Arti di Budapest,* Budapest 1989, no.17). A similar group of figures appears in Agostino's fresco *The Battle of the Romans and Sabines* in the Palazzo Magnani, Bologna (see C. Volpe, *Il fregio dei Carracci e i dipinti di Palazzo Magnani in Bologna,* Bologna 1972).

Jacques Petithory, Paris

10 AGOSTINO CARRACCI
Bologna 1557 - Parma 1602

CEPHALUS AND AURORA.

Bears number: *No.120* and inscription: *Anibal Carraccjo a Rom...a Farne....* Black chalk heightened with white chalk over slight traces of red chalk, on blue paper. On the *verso* studies of feet and a figure in red and black chalk.
282 by 430mm.

Exhibited: Vienna, Albertina, *Die Sammlung Ian Woodner,* 1986, no.28; Munich, Haus der Kunst, *Meisterzeichnungen aus Sechs Jahrhunderten: Die Sammlung Ian Woodner,* 1986, no.28; Madrid, Museo del Prado, *Dibujos de los siglos xiv al xx: Colección Woodner,* 1986/87,no.36; London, Royal Academy of Arts, *Master Drawings: The Woodner Collection,* 1987, no.27; New York, Metropolitan Museum of Art, *Woodner Collection: Master Drawings,* 1990, no.35.

This is a preliminary study for one of the two frescoes which Agostino painted on the ceiling of the Farnese Gallery in the Palazzo Farnese, Rome shortly before 1600 (fig.25). It differs in important respects from the final composition and from the cartoon which is now in the National Gallery, London (see J. Rupert Martin, *The Farnese Gallery,* Princeton 1965, fig.190). The studies on the *verso* have been connected with another sheet of studies in the Louvre which is by Agostino but preparatory for the fresco of *Polyphemus and Acis* which is attributed to Annibale (see Woodner catalogue, *op.cit.).* The handling of chalk and the figure types are strongly reminiscent of Annibale's.

The reputation of the Carracci having been firmly established by their work in several Bolognese palaces, Agostino and Annibale were hired by Cardinal Odoardo Farnese to work on the decoration of the Farnese palace in Rome. Annibale arrived there in 1595 and began work on the Camerino. Agostino arrived in 1597 and joined in the decoration of the Gallery. He seems only to have completed two frescoes (*Cephalus and Aurora* and *Glaucus and Scylla)* before he fell out with Annibale and left Rome. He returned to Bologna and then went to Parma where he was employed by Duke Ranuccio Farnese from July 1600 until his death in 1602.

Dian and Andrea Woodner, New York

11 ANNIBALE CARRACCI
Bologna 1560 - Rome 1609

A DESIGN FOR A WALL DECORATION: IN THE CENTRAL OVAL, EUROPA AND THE BULL.

Bears old attribution in brown ink: *Hannibal Caracio.* Pen and brown ink and wash over red chalk.
141 by 212mm.

Provenance: Nicholas Lanier (L.2886); Lord Arundel; Jonathan Richardson, Snr. (L.2183); Charles Rogers (L.625); Sir Thomas Lawrence (L.2445); Lord Francis Egerton, 1st Earl of Ellesmere (L.2710b) and by descent to the Duke of Sutherland, his sale, London, Sotheby's, 11 July 1972, lot 42; The British Rail Pension Fund, sale, London, Sotheby's, 2 July 1990, lot 49.

Exhibited: London, Lawrence Gallery, Sixth Exhibition, *A Catalogue of One Hundred Original drawings by .... Carracci ....,* 1836, no.91 (as 'one of the ornaments of the Farnese Palace'); London, P.&D. Colnaghi, *Drawings by the Carracci and other Masters,* 1955, no.24; Newcastle upon Tyne, King's College, *The Carracci, Drawings and Paintings,* 1961, no.116.

Literature: *Catalogue of the Ellesmere Collection of Drawings at Bridgewater House,* London 1898, no.31; P.A. Tomory, *The Ellesmere Collection of Old Master Drawings,* Leicester Museum, 1954, no.53, pl.xiii; D. Posner, 'An Unpublished Drawing by Annibale Carracci for the Palazzo Fava Frescoes', *Master Drawings,* vol.4, no.i, 1966, pp.29-31, fig.2; D. Posner, *Annibale Carracci,* New York 1971, vol.ii, under cat. no.14, fig.14a; G. Malafarina, *L'Opera Completa di Annibale Carracci,* Milan 1976, p.89, fig.14^{1}; A. Emiliani *et.al., Bologna 1584,* Bologna 1984, p.88.

This is one of three drawings convincingly related to Annibale's frieze decorations illustrating the story of Europa, painted *circa* 1583/84 in a small room of the Palazzo Fava, Bologna. It shows an early stage in the development of the design, quite different from the final solution. The other two related drawings are a quick sketch in the Uffizi and the very beautiful *Europa and the Bull,* now in a private collection (see D. Posner, *Annibale Carracci,* London 1971, pls.14b, d). See also cat. no.12, which is possibly an even earlier idea for the same commission.

Private Collection

Actual size

12 **ANNIBALE CARRACCI**
Bologna 1560 - Rome 1609

DESIGN FOR A WALL DECORATION: A CARTOUCHE WITH FIGURES IN A LANDSCAPE FLANKED BY TWO CAPTIVES AND A SATYR.

Bears old attribution: *Anibal Carache.* Pen and brown ink and wash over red chalk.
115 by 255mm.

Provenance: Sir Peter Lely (L.2092); William Esdaile (L.2617).

Exhibited: Edinburgh, The Merchants' Hall, *Italian 17th Century Drawings from British Private Collections,* 1972, no.21, illus.

Literature: London, Sotheby's, *The Ellesmere Collection,* 11 July 1972, in note to lot 42.

This drawing was first published in the Edinburgh Festival exhibition as an early idea for the decorations of the *Camerino d'Europa* in the Palazzo Fava. It differs considerably from the scheme as executed, but it can certainly be dated on stylistic grounds to that period of Annibale's activity, around 1583/84. See also cat. no.11.

Private Collection

13 ANNIBALE CARRACCI
Bologna 1560 - Rome 1609

A KNEELING FEMALE FIGURE HOLDING A BANNER, A MAN STANDING BESIDE HER, HOLDING A SHEET OF PAPER.

Red chalk with touches of white chalk, on faded blue paper.
298 by 216mm.

Provenance: John Skippe, by descent to Mrs. Rayner-Wood; Edward Holland-Martin, his sale, Christie's, 20-21 November 1958, lot 229a (as ascribed to Veronese, with a note saying it was more likely to be an eighteenth century drawing, possibly by G.B. Tiepolo); anonymous sale, London, Sotheby's, 21 May 1963, lot 86 (as Giovanni Battista Tiepolo); anonymous sale, London, Sotheby's, 2 July 1990, lot 89 (as Annibale Carracci).

Exhibited: Birmingham, Museum and Art Gallery, *Art Treasures of the Midlands,* 1934, no.205 (as Paolo Veronese, with a note saying bought by John Skippe in Venice in the eighteenth century).

Literature: Birmingham, Alabama, Birmingham Museum of Art and Montgomery Museum, *Veronese and his studio in North American Collections,* 1972, p.60 (as Veronese); Richard Cocke, *Veronese's Drawings,* London 1984, p.361, no.194 (as a rejected attribution to Veronese).

This drawing was traditionally seen as the work of a Venetian artist, either of the 16th century (Veronese) or the 18th century (Tiepolo). The attribution to Annibale was first proposed in the recent Sotheby's sale and has since been accepted by several scholars. The drawing shows strong Venetian influence which is visible in a number of Annibale's early paintings such as the *Crucifixion,* dated 1583, now in S. Maria della Carità, Bologna. Although the drawing cannot be connected to any known work by Annibale, it can be compared stylistically with studies associated with his early career such as one in Budapest related to the Palazzo Poggi frescoes which is executed in red chalk with a very similar *ductus* (see A. Czére, *Disegni di Artisti Bolognesi nel Museo delle Belle Arti di Budapest,* Bologna 1989, no.9).

Private Collection

14 ANNIBALE CARRACCI
Bologna 1560 - Rome 1609

THE ASSUMPTION OF THE VIRGIN.

Pen and brown ink and wash over black chalk heightened with white. Squared in black chalk. Right top and bottom corners made up.
541 by 355mm.

Provenance: Sir Peter Lely (L.2092); William, 2nd Duke of Devonshire (L.718).

Exhibited: Pittsburgh, The Frick Art Museum, and elsewhere, *Old Master Drawings from Chatsworth,* 1987/88, no.17; and then, Cambridge, Fitzwilliam Museum, 1989.

Literature: Jonathan Richardson, *An Account of Some of the Statues, Bas-Reliefs, Drawings and Pictures in Italy etc.,* London 1722, p.343; G. Waagen, *Treasures of Art in Great Britain,* London 1854, iii, p.358 (as Annibale); D. Posner, *Annibale Carracci,* London 1971, vol.ii, p.19, under cat. no.40 (as by a Carracci follower); A.W.A. Boschloo, *Annibale Carracci in Bologna,* The Hague 1974, vol.i, p.14, vol.ii, fig.17 (as Annibale).

In his catalogue of the recent Chatsworth exhibition, Michael Jaffé quite justifiably puts aside Donald Posner's unexplained doubts and reaffirms the traditional view that this very impressive drawing is a preparatory study, with significant differences, for Annibale's altarpiece painted in 1587 for the Confraternity of San Rocco in Reggio Emilia (fig.12). In 1661 the painting was moved to the Ducal Collection in Modena. Jonathan Richardson saw it there on his trip in 1722, and, while referring to it in his *Account* as being by Lodovico, noted that the drawing belonged to the Duke of Devonshire. In 1746 the painting was taken to Dresden, where it still is today. The technique of the Chatsworth drawing makes it similar in tonality and effect to the monochrome oils on paper which are characteristic of many other Bolognese artists such as Faccini (see cat. no.27) and Cavedone.

The Duke of Devonshire and the Chatsworth Settlement Trustees

15 **LODOVICO CARRACCI**
Bologna 1555 - Bologna 1619

A MAN PULLING A ROPE.

Bears old attribution in pen and ink: *di Lodovico Carasa.* Black chalk.
350 by 260mm.

This very impressive chalk study was connected by Bodmer to the somewhat similar figure of a monk drawing water in one of Lodovico's frescoes in San Michele in Bosco. His opinion was repeated by other scholars until the acquisition in 1964 by the Musée de la Chartreuse, Douai, of the painting of *The Flagellation* in which this figure appears (fig.26). Initially the painting was attributed to Annibale, with the assistance of Lodovico, but it was soon firmly attributed to Lodovico himself (both by Rosenberg and Mahon, 1965). There is some variation in the precise dating proposed by various scholars, but most agree that it is a work of the very late 1580s. Babette Bohn also dates the Chatsworth study stylistically to *circa* 1590 and compares it with the *Study of a Serving Girl* in the Uffizi. Of these drawings, she writes 'Lodovico's evolving facility with the figure during the early 1590s was founded on his extensive practice of drawing from life and his conscientious use of detailed preparatory studies for his paintings, both aspects of his working procedure that were at their height during these years'. (B. Bohn, *op.cit.*, p.412).

Provenance: Sir Peter Lely (L.2092); William, 2nd Duke of Devonshire (L.718).

Exhibited: Leeds, *National Exhibition of Works of Art,* 1868, no.2686; London, Royal Academy, *Drawings by Old Masters,* 1953, p.42, no.153; Bologna, Palazzo dell'Archiginnasio, *Mostra dei Carracci: Disegni,* 1956, p.29, no.14, not illus.; Manchester, City Art Gallery, *Old Master Drawings from Chatsworth,* 1961, p.9, no.22, not illus.; Newcastle upon Tyne, King's College, *The Carracci, Drawings and Paintings,* 1961, no.3; Washington, National Gallery of Art, and elsewhere, *Old Master Drawings from Chatsworth,* 1962/63, no.17; London, Royal Academy, *Old Master Drawings from Chatsworth,* 1969, no.17.

(continued)

di lodovico carata

(continued)

Literature: H. Bodmer, *Lodovico Carracci,* Burg bei Magdeburg 1939, p.74; p.148, no.10; pl.126; R. Wittkower, *The Drawings of the Carracci .... at Windsor Castle,* London 1952, p. 101, under no.13; Paris, Louvre, *Le Caravage et la peinture italienne du xvii siècle,* 1965, p.67, under no.31 (entry by C. Gnudi); D. Mahon, 'Stock-Taking in *Seicento* Studies', *Apollo,* vol.82, 1965, p.390, note 7; Paris, Petit Palais, *Le xvie siècle européen,* 1965/66,p.56, under no.69 (entry by Pierre Rosenberg); R. Roli, *I Disegni Italiani del Seicento, Scuole Emiliana ....,* Treviso 1969, p.4, pl.1; Bologna, Palazzo dell'Archiginnasio, *Natura ed espressione nell'arte bolognese-emiliana,* 1970, p.204, under no.56; C. Volpe, 'Sugli inizi di Ludovico Carracci', *Paragone,* 317-319, 1976, p.128, note 22; B. Bohn, 'The Chalk Drawings of Ludovico Carracci', *Master Drawings,* 1984, vol.xxii, no.4, p.411, pl.5; Dunkerque, Musée des Beaux-Arts, and elsewhere, *De Carache à Guardi,* 1985/86, p.63, under no.14; Bologna, Pinacoteca Nazionale, and elsewhere, *The Age of Correggio and the Carracci,* 1986, p.307, under no.107; Paris, Grand Palais, and Milan, Palazzo Reale, *Seicento, le siècle de Caravage dans les Collections françaises,* 1988, p.159, illus.; D. Benati, *Disegni Emiliani del sei-settecento,* 1991, p.15, illus. p.17, no.1.2.

The Duke of Devonshire and the Chatsworth Settlement Trustees

16 LODOVICO CARRACCI
Bologna 1555 - Bologna 1619

A MAN WEARING A HAT AND HOLDING A SWORD.

Bears inscription: *Caracci.* Red chalk heightened with white chalk. Made up to the top right edge and corner.
407 by 180mm.

Provenance: C. Prayer (L.2044); anonymous sale, London, Christie's, 8 December 1987, lot 24.

In the Christie's sale catalogue, Babette Bohn was credited with making the attribution to Lodovico. She dates it *circa* 1589/92and compares it to Lodovico's *Study of a Nude Youth Sleeping* in the Ashmolean Museum, Oxford (see B. Bohn, 'The Chalk Drawings of Ludovico Carracci', *Master Drawings,* 1984, vol.xxii, no.4, pl.11).

Private Collection

17 **LODOVICO CARRACCI**
Bologna 1555 - Bologna 1619

THE APPARITION OF THE 'CRISTO PORTACROCE' TO CARTHUSIAN MONKS.

Pen and brown ink and wash.
362 by 250mm.

Provenance: William, 2nd Duke of Devonshire (L.718).

Exhibited: Pittsburgh, The Frick Art Museum, and elsewhere, *Old Master Drawings from Chatsworth,* 1987/88, no.20; and then, Cambridge, Fitzwilliam Museum, 1989.

Literature: London, Sotheby's, *The Ellesmere Collection, Part I,* 11 July 1972, under lot 4; L. Street, 'La Vendita Ellesmere di Disegni dei Carracci', *Arte Illustrata,* no.50, September 1972, p.356, illus. p.358, fig.12.

As Lenora Street was the first to recognize, this is a preparatory study, with differences, for Lodovico's fresco in the church of S. Gerolamo in the Certosa, Bologna, which survives only as a damaged fragment. Another preparatory study was in the Ellesmere collection; both differ from the fresco in the important respect that there the monks are shown carrying their own crosses, an even more mystical representation than the usual popular Carthusian iconography of the subject (see the painting by Bergognone for the Certosa, Pavia, B. Berenson, *Italian Pictures of the Renaissance, Central Italian and North Italian Schools,* London 1968, vol.iii, fig.1474). Miss Street, although quoted in the Ellesmere sale catalogue as dating Lodovico's fresco *circa* 1589, in her review of the sale (*op.cit.*) decided that for compositional and stylistic reasons 1592 was more convincing (Bodmer had suggested 1593/95). The Chatsworth drawing was formerly attributed to Lionello Spada (1576-1622). Another drawing by Lodovico showing Carthusian monks kneeling and with crosses, adoring an apparition of Christ seated on clouds and holding a cross, was in the collection of Michel Gaud, sold Monaco, Sotheby's, 20 June 1987, lot 101.

The Duke of Devonshire and the Chatsworth Settlement Trustees

18 FRANCESCO CAVAZZONI
Bologna 1559 - Bologna after 1616

ST. CATHERINE BEFORE THE EMPEROR MAXENTIUS.

Pen and brown ink and wash. Squared.
235 by 162mm.

Provenance: William Roscoe, his sale, Liverpool, Winstanley, 23-28 September 1816, lot 104 (as 'Perino del Vaga, *St. Helena avowing her adherence to Christianity,* fine pen and indian ink, Capital'); Henry Blundell.

Literature: A. Ghirardi, 'Francesco Cavazzoni', in Fortunati, 1986, vol.ii, p.854, illus. p.858.

This is a preparatory study for Cavazzoni's altarpiece painted *circa* 1582 for the parish church at Castel S. Pietro, Bologna (fig.16). As Ghirardi notes (*op.cit.*), the painting and the drawing owe much in composition and style to the examples of Prospero Fontana and Orazio Samacchini. The drawing was traditionally attributed to Perino del Vaga. A.E. Popham suggested Marco Pino and then Nosadella, but the correct attribution was made recently by Jürgen Winkelmann.

Cavazzoni's paintings are in the Bolognese Mannerist style of Samacchini and Passerotti (with whom he probably trained). By the end of the sixteenth century, however, he became more closely allied to the Carracci, working with them on the decoration of the ceiling of the Palazzo dei Diamanti at Ferrara. After 1600 he seems to have abandoned painting and pursued scholarly and antiquarian interests, producing, among other publications, an early guide to Bologna and a drawing manual. For further information on the artist, see also R. Varese, *Francesco Cavazzoni, Critico e pittore,* Florence 1969.

Private Collection

19 **BARTOLOMEO CESI**
Bologna 1556 - Bologna 1629

A STANDING DRAPED FIGURE.

Red chalk heightened with traces of white chalk, on blue paper. Made up at the top and at the left edge.
340 by 248mm.

Exhibited: Milan, Stanza del Borgo, *Antichi disegni dal xvi al xix secolo,* 1988, p.18, illus.

Literature: J. Bentini and A. Mazza, *Disegni Emiliani del Sei e Settecento, I grandi cicli di affreschi,* Modena 1990, p.32, no.5.1.

This study, drawn from life, is preparatory for the central figure in Cesi's fresco *An Allegory of Fidelity and Silence* painted in 1590 in the Palazzo Magnani, Bologna (fig.3). A drawing for the whole composition is in the Art Institute, Chicago (see A. Graziani, *Bartolomeo Cesi,* Milan 1988, fig.36). The subject of the painting is an allegory appropriate to the civic duties entailed by Lorenzo Magnani's position as a Gonfaloniere del Popolo (see C. Volpe, *Il fregio dei Carracci e i dipinti di Palazzo Magnani in Bologna,* Bologna 1972).

Private Collection

20 BARTOLOMEO CESI
Bologna 1556 - Bologna 1629

A BOY PLAYING A VIOLA DA GAMBA.

Bears inscription in brown ink: *Agost. Caracci 1591.* Red chalk heightened with white chalk, on blue paper.
234 by 164mm.

Provenance: Baron J.G. Verstolk van Soelen, his sale, Amsterdam, G. Lamberts, 22 March 1847, lot 130 (as Agostino Carracci); Gerard Leembruggen, his sale, Amsterdam, 5 March 1866, lot 907 (as Agostino Carracci); John Malcolm; The Hon. A.E. Gathorne-Hardy; Geoffrey Gathorne-Hardy; The Hon. Robert Gathorne-Hardy, his sale, London, Sotheby's, 24 November 1976, lot 25.

Exhibited: London, Royal Academy, *Drawings by Old Masters,* 1953, no.155; Edinburgh, The Merchants' Hall, *Italian 16th Century Drawings from British Private Collections,* 1969, no.28, pl.64; London, P.&D. Colnaghi, *Loan Exhibition of Drawings by Old Masters from the Collection of Mr. Geoffrey Gathorne-Hardy,* 1971, no.31, pl.xx, and afterwards at the Ashmolean Museum, Oxford.

Literature: *Descriptive catalogue of drawings .... in the possession of the Hon. A.E. Gathorne-Hardy,* Ballantyne Press, 1902, no.20 (as Annibale Carracci); Alberto Graziani, *Bartolomeo Cesi,* Milan 1988, fig.34.

A.E. Popham, at the time of the 1953 Royal Academy exhibition, identified this as a study for the angel musician in the upper right of Cesi's *Adoration of the Magi,* which is the central part of his triptych installed on the altar of S. Domenico, Bologna in August 1595 (fig.4). Two other drawings related to the altarpiece are included in this exhibition (see cat. nos.21 and 22), and three others are known: a chalk study for *God the Father* (Royal Collection, Windsor), another musician (British Museum), and a pen and ink sketch for the *Adoration of the Magi* (Bologna, Pinacoteca Nazionale, fig.1).

Cesi studied first with Nosadella, and his early work shows the influence of Bolognese Mannerists such as Fontana. Later his adherence to the strong Counter-reformation beliefs of the Bolognese Cardinal Paleotti led him towards a greater naturalism, which is particularly evident in his fine chalk drawings, done from life and usually carefully preparatory for paintings such as the present example. It is not surprising that they have frequently been attributed to the Carracci.

Private Collection

Agost. Caracci 1591

21 **BARTOLOMEO CESI**
Bologna 1556 - Bologna 1629

THE MADONNA AND CHILD.

Bears attribution on the old mount: *Lodovico Carracci.* Black chalk heightened with white, on blue paper. Squared in red chalk.
159 by 143mm.

Provenance: St. Germain (according to inscription on the backing); Sir Robert Witt (L.2228b on the mount); Witt Collection (no.2417, as 16th Century Italian School).

Literature: A. Graziani, *Bartolomeo Cesi,* Milan 1988, fig.31; J. Bentini, *Disegni della Galleria Estense di Modena,* Modena 1989, p.278.

This is a study for the Madonna and Child in Cesi's altarpiece in S. Domenico, Bologna (fig.4 and see cat. nos.20 and 22). A copy of these figures drawn by the 19th Century Modenese artist Adeodato Malatesta is in the Galleria Estense, Modena (see Bentini, *op.cit.).*

Courtauld Institute Galleries, London (Witt Collection 2417)

22 **BARTOLOMEO CESI**
Bologna 1556 - Bologna 1629

STUDY OF A STANDING MAN HOLDING A JAR.

Red chalk heightened with white chalk, on faded blue paper.
338 by 144mm.

Provenance: Benno Geiger; Henry Oppenheimer, his sale, London, Christie's, 10-14 July 1936, lot 60A (as Annibale Carracci); anonymous sale, London, Sotheby's, 4 July 1988, lot 30 (as Bartolomeo Cesi).

This is a study for the figure of one of the Magi in Cesi's altarpiece in S. Domenico, Bologna (fig.4). In the pen and ink study for the whole composition (fig.1) the pose of the king is very similar, but in the painting it is somewhat changed. See also cat. nos.20 and 21.

Private Collection

23 **BARTOLOMEO CESI**
Bologna 1556 - Bologna 1629

A CARTHUSIAN MONK.

Bears inscription on the old mount: *Stava notato per Fr. Vanni ma io lo credo piùtosto d'/Agostino Caracci.* Pen and brown ink and wash over red chalk. Squared in red chalk.
283 by 130mm.

Provenance: Earl of Cholmondeley; Jonathan Richardson, Snr. (L.2184, and his shelf mark); John Barnard (L.1420); Samuel Woodburn; Sir Robert Witt; Witt Collection (no.1157, as Lodovico Carracci).

Literature: C. Johnston, *Mostra di disegni bolognesi dal xvi al xviii secolo,* Florence 1973, p.33, under no.17; J. Byam Shaw, *The Italian Drawings of the Frits Lugt Collection,* Paris 1983, vol.i, p.334, under no.329, illus. fig.91; A. Graziani, *Bartolomeo Cesi,* Milan 1988, fig.44.

This is a study for one of the figures of Carthusian saints and *beati* which Cesi painted to the right of the entrance arch to the choir chapel in S. Gerolamo in the Certosa, Bologna (fig.2). Cesi's work in the choir (which included frescoes and three paintings) is generally dated between 1612 and 1616, although D. Benati (in *Paragone,* 1980, pp.3-28) has suggested an earlier dating of 1595 to 1600. Numerous other drawings related to the commission have survived.

Courtauld Institute Galleries, London (Witt Collection 1157)

24 PIETRO FACCINI
Bologna 1562? - Bologna 1602

ULYSSES AND THE SIRENS.

Red chalk with stumping and some red wash. A black ink sketch on the *verso.*
257 by 360mm.

Exhibited: London, Yvonne Tan Bunzl, *Old Master Drawings,* 1987, no.20.

The attribution to Faccini was first made by Nicholas Turner, and is convincing although there is little among his surviving works with which to compare it. As Yvonne Tan Bunzl writes in her catalogue, the closest comparison is with *The Judgment of Paris,* now in the Fogg Art Museum, which has been variously attributed to Annibale Carracci and to Bartolomeo Schedone but which Mario di Giampaolo believes to be by Faccini (see M. Cazort and C. Johnston, *Bolognese Drawings in North American Collections,* Ottawa 1982, no.26). The sketch on the *verso* is after the figure of Christ in a painting by Barocci, an artist whose work influenced Faccini. This must be a work of the 1580s when Faccini was working with the Carracci.

Private Collection

25 PIETRO FACCINI
Bologna 1562? - Bologna 1602

Recto: STANDING MALE NUDE SEEN IN PROFILE, AND STUDIES OF FEET AND AN ARM;
Verso: STUDIES OF HEADS.

Black chalk, heightened with white chalk (*recto);* pen and brown ink and black chalk (*verso).*
560 by 354mm.

Provenance: Anonymous sale, New York, Sotheby's, 13 January 1988, lot 29.

This is characteristic of Faccini's male nudes in its exaggerated forms and in the study of the play of light over the body. The quick sketches of heads on the *verso* reveal a less familiar aspect of his draughtsmanship (fig.5). Although Faccini worked with the Carracci, his personality seems to have been strong and eccentric and he broke away from them, pursuing a more individual and pictorial style. His work was admired by his contemporaries as well as by Malvasia who praises him in particular for his imagination and spirit. Cardinal Leopoldo de'Medici collected many of his drawings, particulary studies of nudes, which are now in the Uffizi (see, for example, Mario di Giampaolo, *Disegni Emiliani del Rinascimento,* Modena 1989, p.302). See also cat. no.26.

Jak Katalan, New York

26 **PIETRO FACCINI**
Bologna 1562? - Bologna 1602

STUDY OF A MALE NUDE HOLDING A PIECE OF DRAPERY.

Bears number: *56*. Red chalk.
414 by 267mm.

Provenance: Said to be part of a dismembered album from the collection of Filippo Baldinucci (1624/1696); anonymous sale, New York, Sotheby's, 12 January 1990, lot 22.

Following his break with the Carracci, Faccini started his own academy in competition with theirs. He, too, concentrated on studies from the nude model. A red chalk study comparable to this one is among the large group of Faccini drawings at Modena (see J. Bentini, *Disegni della Galleria Estense di Modena,* Modena 1989, p.216). Another important group of nude studies is in Berlin. See also cat. no.25.

Private Collection

56

27 PIETRO FACCINI
Bologna 1562? - Bologna 1602

Recto: SUPPLICANTS BEFORE AN ALTAR;

Verso: STUDIES OF FIGURES FOR THE SAME COMPOSITION.

Drawn with the point of the brush in pink and white oil over pen and brown ink, on paper washed brown. Top corners made up.
288 by 516mm.

Provenance: Bears unidentified collector's mark (L.2781); W. Bates (L.2604); Herbert List (bears his dry stamp); anonymous sale, London, Christie's, 1 July 1986, lot 84 (as Giacomo Cavedone).

Exhibited: New York, P.&D. Colnaghi, *Old Master Drawings,* 1987, no.15 (as Faccini, with a catalogue entry by Mario di Giampaolo).

Luca Baroni recognized this as the work of Faccini. It has not been connected with a known commission. Faccini experimented with a variety of media throughout his life, and was particularly interested in the monochromatic possibilities of oil on paper. This example probably dates from the 1590s when he seems to have been influenced by Venetian painting, in particular the work of Tintoretto. *Verso* illustrated fig.6.

Private Collection

28 **PIETRO FACCINI**
Bologna 1562? - Bologna 1602

THE MEETING AT THE GOLDEN GATE, WITH FOUR PROPHETS BELOW.

Pen and brown ink and wash heightened with white, on paper washed light brown.
573 by 395mm.

Provenance: Sir Thomas Lawrence (L.2445); Matthew Bloxham.

The subject of this drawing is uncertain. Elizabeth McGrath has suggested it may more precisely represent the Conception of the Virgin, for an alter dedicated to the Immaculate Conception. It is a fine example of another facet of Faccini's draughtsmanship. The febrile pen outline and the use of wash to create effects of light can be found in other such compositional studies, some of which are related to recorded works (see, for example, *The Raising of Lazarus,* now in the Louvre, reproduced D. Posner, 'Pietro Faccini and the Carracci', *Paragone,* 131, 1960, pl.40). A drawing for the figures in the upper part of the composition is in a private collection.

Private Collection

29 LAVINIA FONTANA
Bologna 1552 - Rome 1614

THE CRUCIFIXION WITH ST. JEROME AND TWO PATRONS.

Black chalk and pen and brown ink heightened with white chalk, on faded blue paper. Squared in black chalk.
519 by 342mm.

Provenance: Sir John Witt (L.646a on the mount), his sale, London, Sotheby's, 19 February 1987, lot 231 (as School of the Marche, Sixteenth Century).

Exhibited: London, Courtauld Institute Galleries, *The John Witt Collection,* 1963, no.15 (as Sebastiano del Piombo).

This very finished drawing is a preparatory study, with some differences, for a damaged altarpiece now stored in the Palazzo Pepoli, Bologna (fig.18). Maria Teresa Cantaro believes it to be the painting by Lavinia Fontana which Malvasia describes in the Baldi Chapel, S. Bernardino, Bologna (see M.T. Cantaro, *Lavinia Fontana bolognese,* Milan 1989, p.140, illus.). The drawing is an important addition to the few attributed to Lavinia Fontana, most of which are small portraits. This is the first compositional study which can be connected to a painting traditionally attributed to her.

At the time of going to press we have discovered that the present drawing has been independently connected to the painting and published with an attribution to Calvaert (see A. Mazza, *La Collezione dei Dipinti Antichi della Cassa di Risparmio di Cesena,* Ferrara 1991, p.65, illus.).

Private Collection

30 PROSPERO FONTANA
Bologna 1512 - Bologna 1597

Recto: NEMESIS AND ADRASTUS;

Verso: TIME AND A YOUNG MAN AT A TABLE.

Pen and brown ink and wash.
122 by 90mm.

This and the following two drawings are from a series of eighty-four designs, previously bound together in an album which was sold London, Sotheby's, 13 July 1972, lot 23. The drawings were engraved by Giulio Bonasone for some of the one hundred and fifty plates illustrating Achille Bocchi's *Symbolicarum Quaestionum de Universo Genere quas serio ludebat, Libri Quinque,* published in Bologna in 1555. Other drawings from the series are in the British Museum (see J.A. Gere and P. Pouncey, *Italian Drawings, Artists working in Rome c.1550-1640,* London 1983, pp.78-79, illus.), and elsewhere. The prints after these two designs, nos. lxv and lxvi, are engraved in the same direction (*Illustrated Bartsch,* vol.29, p.75, no.244, p.76, no.245).

Formerly thought to be by Bonasone himself, the drawings from this album were reattributed to Prospero Fontana by John Gere and Philip Pouncey (*op.cit.*), following Malvasia who, in the *Felsina Pittrice,* described Fontana as being responsible for many of the designs for Bocchi's book. Most of the eighty-four drawings are done in the same technique of delicate pen and ink and wash and are of roughly the same size. Pouncey and Gere noted their 'sophisticated if at times rather superficial elegance' which they found hard to reconcile with Bonasone's more clumsy and provincial character. This, combined with the Florentine traits evident in the designs, reinforces the attribution to Fontana who worked with Vasari and would have encountered Salviati whose influence is particularly visible. Slight variations of style among the drawings indicate that they may not all be by the same hand (see cat. nos.31 and 32). Adalgisa Lugli, who has written an article on the importance of Bocchi's book and its place in the intellectual life of Bologna, believes all the drawings are by Bonasone (see 'Le *Symbolicae Quaestiones* di Achille Bocchi e la cultura dell'emblema in Emilia', in A. Emiliani, *Le Arti a Bologna e in Emilia dal xvi al xvii secolo,* Bologna 1982, pp.87-96).

Private Collection

Recto actual size

Verso actual size

31 BOLOGNESE SCHOOL, 16TH CENTURY

PRUDENCE AND GOODNESS HOLDING THE COAT OF ARMS OF CARDINAL OTTO TRUCHSESS VON WALDBURG.

Pen and brown ink and grey wash.
112 by 84mm.

See note to cat. no.30. This is the design, in the same direction but without some of the inscriptions, for pl.cxxix (*Illustrated Bartsch,* vol.29, p.107, no.308). The figure types are reminiscent of the work of Nicolò dell'Abate.

Otto Truchsess was a German who came to Bologna and studied law at the University with Ugo Boncompagni, later Pope Gregory XIII (see cat. no.41). He became a favourite of Pope Paul III who made him a cardinal in 1544. He was very active in religious affairs in Italy and in Germany, a supporter of the Jesuits, of religious reforms, and of the Council of Trent. He also appears to have been a patron of art as he commissioned Tibaldi to decorate a chapel in the basilica at Loreto, for which initial payments are recorded on 22 November 1553 (see F. da Morrovalle, *Arte Antica e Moderna,* 27, 1964, pp.356ff.).

Private Collection

Actual size

32 BOLOGNESE SCHOOL, 16TH CENTURY

A WINGED GENIUS HOLDING A SCROLL WITH A REBUS.

Pen and brown ink and wash.
111 by 80mm.

See note to cat. no.30. This is the design, in the same direction, for plate cxlv (*Illustrated Bartsch,* vol.29, p.115, no.324). The drawing does not seem to be by the same hand as either of the other two included in this exhibition. Some of the hieroglyphs which appear on this page can also be found in illustrations to an early edition of the *Hypnerotomachia Poliphili,* a very popular novel first published in Venice in 1499 (see Frankfurt am Main, Liebieghaus, *Natur und Antike in der Renaissance,* 1985/86, pp.228-229).

Private Collection

Actual size

33 **GIROLAMO SELLARI, called GIROLAMO DA CARPI**
Ferrara circa 1501 - Ferrara circa 1556

THE FLIGHT OF DAEDALUS AND ICARUS.

Bears inscription: *Rosso Fiorentino.* Pen and brown ink and wash heightened with white, on paper washed brown. Made up from two pieces of paper and laid down.
380 by 392mm.

Provenance: Hugh and April Squire, their sale, London, Sotheby's, 28 June 1979, lot 61 (as Biagio Pupini).

In the 1979 sale catalogue entry, an attribution to Girolamo da Carpi was suggested, which now seems convincing on the basis of the figure types and the treatment of the landscape, even though the technique is more obviously reminiscent of Pupini's work. Girolamo was born in Ferrara where he trained with his father and with Garofalo. In 1525 he is recorded at work with Pupini in S. Michele in Bosco in Bologna, and the two artists seem to have been closely associated over the ensuing ten years, both in Bologna and Ferrara. In 1549, Girolamo worked in Rome for both Cardinal Ippolito d'Este and Pope Julius III as an architect and adviser. He returned to Ferrara in 1553 where he continued to work for the d'Este family. The present drawing cannot be connected with any surviving work, but most probably it was for one of the many commissions he received for decorative schemes in the palaces of his patrons. His painting style reflects his training with Garofalo, as well as the influence of Raphael, probably absorbed on an early trip to Rome, and of Parmigianino who came to Bologna in 1527.

Private Collection, Paris

34 **GIROLAMO DA TREVISO**
Treviso circa 1497 - Boulogne 1544

ST. JEROME AND ST. CATHERINE OF ALEXANDRIA.

Bears old attribution on the mount: *Pellegrino da Bologna,* and on the backing: *pellegrini Tibaldi eleve de Daniel de Voltere/ne a Boulogne 1522 mort en 1592.* Pen and brown ink and wash heightened with white.
243 by 220mm.

Provenance: Monsignor Marchetti; Padre Resta; John, Lord Somers (L.2981, bears his number *l.182,* listed in the Lansdowne manuscript as Giovanni de'Vecchi); Sir Joshua Reynolds (L.2364); anonymous sale, London, Christie's, 10 April 1985, lot 25 (as Attributed to Pellegrino Tibaldi).

Philip Pouncey recognized this as a work by Girolamo da Treviso when it appeared for sale in 1985. Mario di Giampaolo has recently suggested that it may be a preparatory study, with some differences, for the lower part of the *Madonna and Child in Glory with Sts. Jerome and Catherine of Alexandria* now in the Narodowe Muzeum, Warsaw (fig.21). Vasari, in his life of Girolamo, writes: *Fece una tavola .... a San Salvatore, ed un altra con la Nostra Donna in aria con alcuni fanciulli, ed ai piè San Ieronimo e Santa Caterina;* .... (see Vasari, *Le Vite,* Milanesi ed., vol.v, p.137). The painting was in the Belloni chapel in San Salvatore, Bologna until the mid-nineteenth century.

Girolamo worked in Treviso and Venice before coming to Bologna where he was well established by 1523. He continued to work primarily in Bologna until he moved to England in 1538. He became a military architect to Henry VIII, and died at the seige of Boulogne.

Private Collection

Pellegrino da Bologna

35 **INNOCENZO FRANCUCCI, called INNOCENZO DA IMOLA**
Imola circa 1490 - Bologna circa 1545

STANDING DRAPED MALE FIGURE, LEANING FORWARD.

Black chalk heightened with white.
215 by 87mm.

Provenance: Johann Georg, Prince of Saxony.

Literature: P. Pouncey, 'Drawings by Innocenzo da Imola', *Master Drawings,* vol.vii, no.3 (1969), p.290, no.7, pl.21; Daniela Ferriani, 'Innocenzo Francucci detto da Imola', in Fortunati, 1986, vol.i, p.65.

As Philip Pouncey was the first to note, this is a study for the figure of St. Joseph in Innocenzo's altarpiece *The Madonna and Child with Saints,* in San Giacomo, Bologna, which is signed and dated 1536 (fig.17). A study for the figure of St. John the Evangelist in the same painting is also in the Scholz collection (Pouncey, *op.cit.,* no.8, pl.22).

Innocenzo seems to have had his early training in Bologna, possibly with Francesco Francia, and then, more extensively, in Florence, probably with Mariotto Albertinelli. After a short return to Imola, he settled in Bologna where he received commissions in the church and monastery of S. Michele in Bosco between 1517 and 1525. He worked in Faenza in the late 1520s, but returned to Bologna where he continued to fulfill important religious and private commissions, including a series of frescoes with mythological subjects for the palace of Cardinal Bonifacio Ferreri. Although he absorbed the influence of Raphael and of Girolamo da Carpi and Parmigianino, it is his early Florentine training which left the most profound impression on his painting.

The Janos Scholz Collection, The Pierpont Morgan Library, New York

36 **GIULIO MORINA**
Bologna 1555/60- Mirandola? 1609

THREE KNEELING SAINTS: ST. FRANCIS, A DEACON, AND A BISHOP (POSSIBLY ST. NICHOLAS).

Pen and brown ink over traces of black chalk.
233 by 196mm.

The attribution of this previously unpublished drawing was made by Mr. Claude Kühn on the basis of comparison with a signed drawing by the artist in Budapest (see A. Czére, *Disegni di Artisti Bolognesi nel Museo delle Belle Arti di Budapest,* Bologna 1989, no.3). According to Malvasia, Morina was a pupil of Sabatini, but also worked extensively in Parma. The group of his paintings reproduced in Daniela Ferriani's article in Vera Fortunati Pietrantonio's *Pittura Bolognese del '500* reflects those influences, together with an intense religious sentiment. The present drawing cannot be connected with any surviving work, but Morina was a prolific artist and Malvasia records many paintings which are now lost. This drawing shows the influence of Passerotti's graphic style. The town in the background does not seem to be Bologna, so this study may have been for a commission in another city.

Private Collection

37 **GIOVANNI FRANCESCO BEZZI, called NOSADELLA**
Bologna documented 1549 - Bologna 1571

Recto and *verso:* THE ANNUNCIATION.

Pen and brown ink and wash and red chalk over traces of black chalk (*recto* and *verso*).
210 by 155mm.

Provenance: Yvonne ffrench, 1963 (as Nicolò Circignani); Sir John Witt (L.646a), his sale, London, Sotheby's, 19 February 1987, lot 230 (as Pellegrino Tibaldi).

Literature: *Illustrated London News,* 2 November 1963, reproduced in a review of Miss ffrench's exhibition; J. Winkelmann, 'Giovanni Francesco Bezzi, detto il Nosadella', in Fortunati, 1986, vol.ii, p.460, illus. p.467.

This is a preparatory study, with differences, for Nosadella's painting which is now in the Art Museum, Princeton University (fig.7). Very little is known about Nosadella's life and works. Only two documented paintings survive, which provide the basis for attributions. As Winkelmann points out, the paintings which are considered early works show the influence of Raphael and also of Polidoro da Caravaggio, which indicates he probably was trained in Rome. His later works are more closely allied with the style of Pellegrino Tibaldi, and have often been attributed to that artist. Winkelmann (*op.cit.,* p.460) dates the Princeton painting around 1565 and, while pointing out that it was attributed to Agostino Carracci in the seventeenth century and more recently to Tibaldi, considers it 'perhaps one of the most original creations of Bolognese Mannerism' and typical of Nosadella's work. The attribution is reinforced by the connection with the present drawing which in its delicate use of line and wash resembles other autograph studies. *Verso* illustrated fig.8.

Private Collection

38 **Attributed to GIOVANNI FRANCESCO BEZZI, called NOSADELLA**
Bologna documented 1549 - Bologna 1571

A SEATED WOMAN SURROUNDED BY CHILDREN, PROBABLY AN ALLEGORY OF CHARITY.

Pen and black ink and grey wash. Pricked for transfer.
197 by 143mm.

Provenance:
Anonymous sale, London, Sotheby's, 21 March 1988, lot 339 (as Follower of Perino del Vaga).

Although previously this drawing has been seen as related to the work of Perino del Vaga, the more recent suggestion that it is comparable to the style of Nosadella seems convincing. The eccentric figure types and the use of wash recall his work.

Private Collection

Actual size

39 **BARTOLOMEO PASSEROTTI**
Bologna 1529 - Bologna 1592

STUDIES FOR THE ADORATION OF THE MAGI.

Bears inscription: *Baccio Bandinelli.* Pen and brown ink and grey wash over black chalk. Made up along the top by a later hand.
430 by 562mm.

Provenance:
General J. Guise.

Exhibited:
Washington, D.C., National Gallery of Art, and elsewhere, *Old Master Drawings from Christ Church, Oxford,* 1972/73, no.52; Washington, D.C., National Gallery of Art and Parma, Galleria Nazionale, *Correggio and his Legacy,* 1984, no.109; Cambridge, Fitzwilliam Museum, *Baccio Bandinelli,* 1988, no.47.

Literature:
J. Byam Shaw, *Drawings by Old Masters at Christ Church, Oxford,* Oxford 1976, vol.i, p.238, no.894, pl.543; M. di Giampaolo and S. Béguin, *Maestri Emiliani del Secondo Cinquecento,* Florence 1979, p.34; A. Ghirardi, *Bastianino. La pittura a Ferrara nel secondo Cinquecento,* Bologna 1985, p.67; C. Höper, *Bartolomeo Passarotti,* Worms 1987, vol.ii, p.177, Z279, fig.23b; A. Ghirardi, *Bartolomeo Passerotti,* Rimini 1990, p.149, fig.2a.

This is a sheet of preparatory studies for the figures of the three Magi in Passerotti's altarpiece now in the Palazzo Arcivescovile, Bologna, but formerly on the Ambrosini altar in the crypt of S. Pietro, Bologna (fig.10). Ghirardi dates the painting around 1564, although some scholars have placed it ten years later, and others somewhat earlier, around 1560, soon after Passerotti's return from Rome. Roger Ward (Cambridge, exhib. cat., *op.cit.*), points out that a considerable number of Passerotti's drawings have been attributed to Bandinelli, probably because of the similarity of their pen styles. The Christ Church study combines Passerotti's familiar energetic penwork with an unusually delicate use of wash.

The Governing Body, Christ Church, Oxford (JBS 894)

40 BARTOLOMEO PASSEROTTI
Bologna 1529 - Bologna 1592

THREE STUDIES OF HANDS.

Pen and brown ink over black chalk, on buff paper.
404 by 270mm.

Provenance: Robert Avelot. From the Pollard-Urquhart Album; anonymous sale, London, Sotheby's, 4 July 1975, lot 19; John Wisdom;

Literature: A. Ghirardi, *Bartolomeo Passerotti,* Rimini 1990, p.171; p.172, note 10; p.174, fig.21d.

As Ghirardi notes (*op.cit.),* Passerotti used two of the studies of hands on this page for the figure of St. Dominic in one of his most important altarpieces, *The Madonna in Glory with St. Petronius, St. Dominic and the Martyrdom of St. Peter Martyr,* painted between 1570 and 1575 for the Butchers' Chapel in S. Petronio, Bologna, where it still hangs (fig.9). The butchers and the notaries were the only two guilds to have their own chapels in S. Petronio, proof of their importance to the life of the city. St. Dominic is the patron saint of butchers, and Ghirardi points out (*op.cit.,* p.171) that the way in which St. Peter Martyr is killed in the background may be an allusion to the butchers' methods of slaughtering animals. A number of other preparatory drawings for the painting are known.

Jan and Marie-Anne Krugier

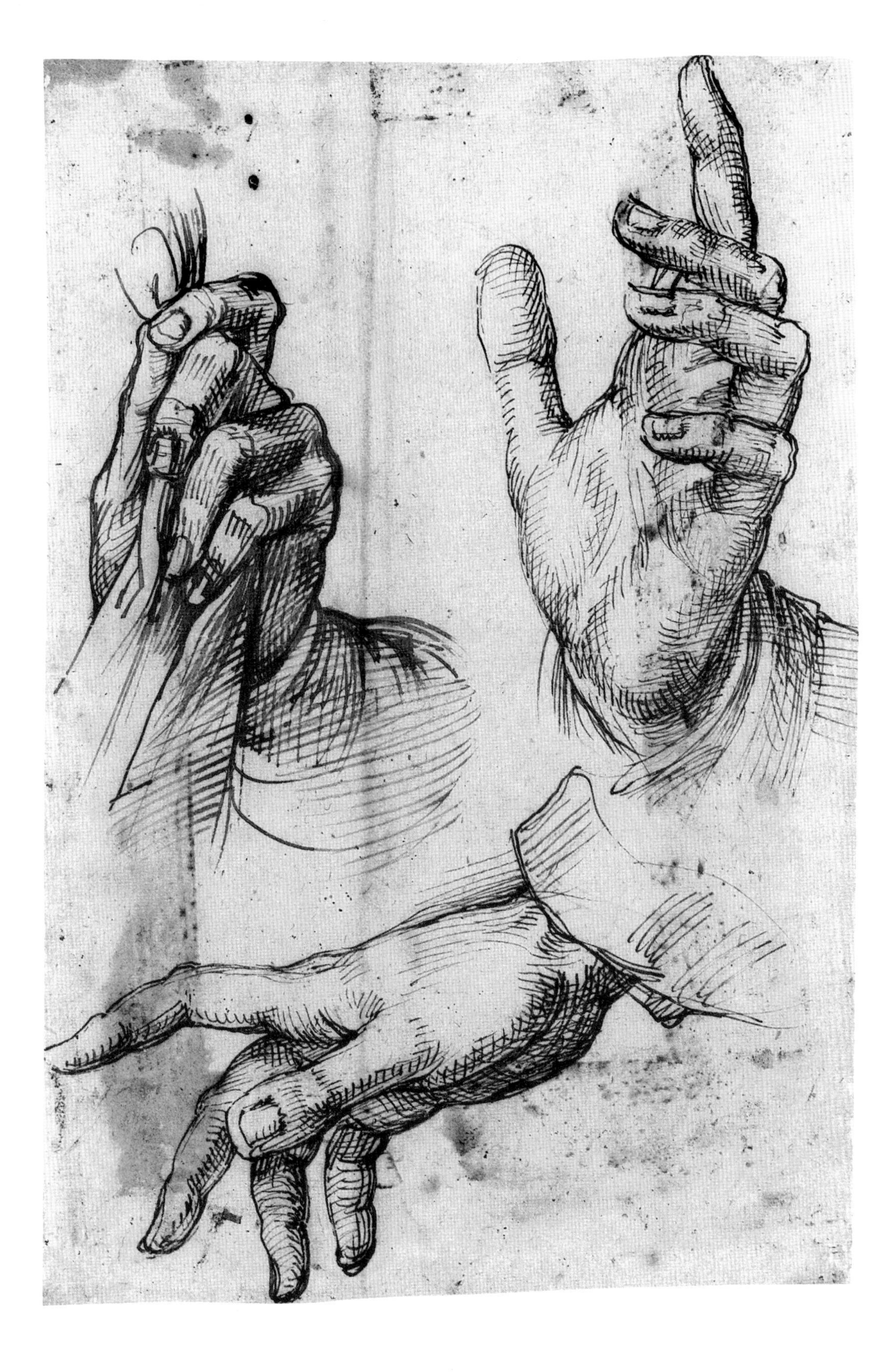

41 **BARTOLOMEO PASSEROTTI**
Bologna 1529 - Bologna 1592

POPE GREGORY XIII SEATED, HIS HAND RAISED IN BLESSING.

Pen and brown ink. Laid down and made up at the top corners.
385 by 254mm.

Provenance: Earl Spencer (L.1530), his sale, London, T. Philipe, 10 June 1811, lot 277; William Esdaile (L.2617, inscribed by him on the back of the mount: *Lord Spencer's coll. 1811 WE P74 N277.* and *Bartolomeo Passarotti, Sch. of Jac. Vignola/painted Hist and Portraits, lived at Rome/florished in 1576.* and his shelf mark: *Q No. 9),* his sale, London, Christie's, 19 June 1840, lot 334, described as 'a noble design in pen'; Artemis Fine Arts U.K. Ltd.; anonymous sale, New York, Sotheby's, 13 January 1989, lot 104.

Literature: Artemis Fine Arts U.K. Ltd., *Master Prints and Drawings, 16th to 19th Centuries,* London 1984.

The Bolognese prelate, Ugo Boncompagni, became Pope Gregory XIII in 1572. Borghini records that Passerotti painted a portrait of him, which Ghirardi has identified in the collection of the Museen der Stadt, Gotha (see A. Ghirardi, *Bartolomeo Passerotti,* Rimini 1990, p.179, no.25). He also drew an allegorical portrait of the Pope which was engraved by Domenico Tibaldi. The present drawing is made after Alessandro Menganti's bronze statue of Gregory XIII, executed in 1580 for the façade of the Palazzo Comunale, Bologna, where it still can be seen today. As the drawing shows the statue in profile, it must have been drawn before the statue was placed *in situ.*

Private Collection

42 **BARTOLOMEO PASSEROTTI**
Bologna 1529 - Bologna 1592

THE BONCOMPAGNI DRAGON.

Pen and brown ink over black chalk. Left side made up.
361 by 440mm.

This dragon, the Boncompagni family emblem, was certainly executed in connection with a commission for Pope Gregory XIII (see cat. no.41).

Private Collection

43 **BARTOLOMEO PASSEROTTI**
Bologna 1529 - Bologna 1592

HEAD OF A DEMON.

Bears number: *229* and inscription: *Passerotti.* Pen and brown ink.
415 by 280mm.

Provenance: Anonymous sale, London, Sotheby's, 25 June 1970, lot 37; Alister Mathews; Dr. and Mrs. Malcolm Bick; anonymous sale, London, Sotheby's, 2 July 1984, lot 3.

Exhibited: Hartford, Conn., Wadsworth Atheneum, *One Hundred Master Drawings from New England Private Collections,* 1973, no.7.

This energetic and vivid image incorporates two important strains in Passerotti's art: his interest in the scientific and natural world, and also in the grotesque. By the mid-sixteenth century, Bologna had become a centre of scientific study, due in part to the presence at the University of Ulisse Aldrovandi who published various books on the animal world. He and Passerotti were friends and fellow collectors of natural specimens and curiosities. Passerotti's own collection contained paintings, sculptures, cameos and drawings, and was much visited and admired by his contemporaries. This interest in the natural world, and in anatomy, is reflected not only in his fine portraits, but also in his vigorous genre paintings of fruit sellers and butchers and in the slightly more exaggerated grotesque figure groups found in some of his paintings and drawings. The present demon is a product of those interests, carried into the realm of fantasy. It does not seem to be related to a painting.

Private Collection

44 **FRANCESCO PRIMATICCIO**
Bologna 1504 - Fontainebleau 1570

A STANDING DRAPED MALE FIGURE.

Bears old attribution and numbering: *Primatizio; 99.* Red chalk heightened with white, on paper tinted pink.
244 by 114mm.

Provenance: P.J. Mariette (L.1852, and on his mount); Pierre Defer; Henri Dumesnil (L.739), his sale, Paris, Hôtel Drouot, 10-12 May 1900, lot 240.

Little is known of Primaticcio's early training - some sources suggest he studied with Innocenzo da Imola and Bagnacavallo, but Vasari does not. He worked with Giulio Romano at the Palazzo del Te in Mantua in the late 1520s and then went to France around 1530 to work for François I at Fontainebleau. He continued to work at the French court for the rest of his life, becoming chief designer at the death of Rosso Fiorentino in 1540. He was in Italy in 1539, making casts of antique statues for François I, and again in 1563 when he met Vasari in Bologna. Although he is often classified as a French artist, Diane De Grazia writes: 'His style remained Italian throughout his years in France, however, and his drawings can be understood best in relation to his Italian upbringing .... He combines the grace and elegance of Correggio and Parmigianino, the strength and volume of Giulio Romano, and the mannered oddity of Rosso in order to create a style of decorative charm that was the basis of French courtly art in the second half of the sixteenth century' (D. De Grazia, *Correggio and his Legacy,* Washington 1984, p.235). The fact that many of Primaticcio's drawings are inscribed *Bologne* also indicates that his contemporaries thought of him as Bolognese. This drawing has not as yet been connected with a known work. It was probably intended as a caryatid figure in a decorative scheme.

Private Collection, Paris

PRIMATIZIO 99

45 **FRANCESCO PRIMATICCIO**
Bologna 1504 - Fontainebleau 1570

ALEXANDER AND CAMPASPE IN THE STUDIO OF APELLES.

Pen and brown ink and pink wash heightened with white. Squared in black chalk. Oval.
349 by 246mm.

Provenance: N.A. Flinck (L.959); William, 2nd Duke of Devonshire (L.718).

Exhibited: Pittsburg, The Frick Art Museum, and elsewhere, *Old Master Drawings from Chatsworth,* 1987/88, no.60; and then Cambridge, Fitzwilliam Museum, 1989.

Literature: L. Dimier, *Le Primatice,* Paris 1900, p.472, no.241; S. Béguin, *et.al., L'Ecole de Fontainebleau,* Paris 1972, p.293, under no.358.

This is the preparatory drawing for one of the small oval compositions on the wall of the *Chambre de Madame d'Estampes* at Fontainebleau, decorated by Primaticcio between 1541 and 1544 with stories from the life of Alexander. The room was transformed into a staircase by Louis XV, but this composition survives, although it was repainted in the nineteenth century. It was engraved several times by artists of the School of Fontainebleau.

The Duke of Devonshire and the Chatsworth Settlement Trustees

46 FRANCESCO PRIMATICCIO
Bologna 1504 - Fontainebleau 1570

A SHEET OF STUDIES: A STOOPING FIGURE IN A SPANDREL, A WOMAN FACING RIGHT.

Red chalk heightened with white.
225 by 192mm.

Provenance: R.H. Randall Davies (L.2903a); Hugh and April Squire, their sale, London, Sotheby's, 28 June 1979, lot 12.

The attribution of this drawing was first made by A.E. Popham. It is a preparatory study for the figures of Philomen and Baucis in the spandrel *Jupiter and Mercury in the Home of Philomen and Baucis,* in the Ballroom at Fontainebleau. Many of Primaticcio's drawings relating to the project are known (see S. Béguin *et. al., L'Ecole de Fontainebleau,* Paris 1972, nos.162-170). The room was painted between 1552/56, primarily by Nicolò dell'Abate working from Primaticcio's designs. The frescoes were recorded in the seventeenth century in prints by Alexandre Bettou (see Robert Dumesnil, *Le peintre-graveur français,* vol.viii).

Private Collection

47 **BIAGIO PUPINI, called DALLE LAME**
Recorded in Bologna 1511-1575

CHRIST WASHING THE DISCIPLES' FEET.

Pen and brown ink and wash heightened with white.
233 by 393mm.

Provenance: Jonathan Richardson, Snr. (L.2184); Hans Calmann.

Exhibited: London, P.&D. Colnaghi, *Old Master Drawings,* 1982, no.40, pl.viii.

Pupini is said to have been a pupil of Francesco Francia, but he is first recorded working with the elder Bagnacavallo at Faenza. Later he collaborated with Girolamo da Carpi both in Bologna and Ferrara. Few of his paintings have survived, but many drawings have. The present sheet is characteristic of his graphic style which has been admirably described by Popham: 'His lively assemblages of small figures, often in front of elaborate architectural backgrounds, are very similar to Polidoro's. Characteristics which mark most of the drawings attributed to Pupini are a cream-coloured or yellow or grey ground, a liberal heightening in rather chalky white, and a general carelessness and lack of precision in the drawing'. (A.E. Popham and J. Wilde, *The Italian Drawings of the XV and XVI Centuries .... at Windsor Castle,* London 1949, p.306, under no.781).

Private Collection

48 **BIAGIO PUPINI, called DALLE LAME**
Recorded in Bologna 1511-1575

THE ADORATION OF THE MAGI.

Pen and brown ink and wash heightened with white, on blue paper. The top corners made up.
225 by 205mm.

Provenance: Jonathan Richardson, Snr. (L.2184 and his attribution on the mount: *Biaggio Bologneso.);* Sir Thomas Lawrence; Sir J.C. Robinson (L.1433 and L.2141b); John Malcolm; The Hon. A.E. Gathorne-Hardy; Geoffrey Gathorne-Hardy; The Hon. Robert Gathorne-Hardy, his sale, London, Sotheby's, 24 November 1976, lot 15.

Exhibited: Edinburgh, The Merchants' Hall, *Italian 16th Century Drawings from British Private Collections,* 1969, no.71, pl.36; London, P.&D. Colnaghi, *Loan Exhibition of Drawings by Old Masters from the Collection of Mr. Geoffrey Gathorne-Hardy,* 1971, no.23, pl.xvii, and afterwards at the Ashmolean Museum, Oxford; Munich, Staatliche Graphische Sammlung, and elsewhere, *Stiftung Ratjen, Italienische Zeichnungen des 16.-18. Jahrhunderts,* 1977/78, no.66.

Literature: J.C. Robinson, *Descriptive Catalogue of drawings by the Old Masters, forming the Collection of John Malcolm of Poltalloch, Esq.,* Chiswick Press 1869, no.231; *Descriptive catalogue of drawings .... in the possession of the Hon. A.E. Gathorne-Hardy,* Ballantyne Press 1902, no.19.

This drawing cannot be connected with a surviving or recorded work. Other drawings of the subject are at Windsor (see A.E. Popham and J. Wilde, *The Italian Drawings ....,* 1949, no.782, pl.98) and at Chatsworth (see A.M. Fioravanti Baraldi in Fortunati, 1986, vol.i, p.195).

Stiftung Ratjen, Vaduz

49 **BIAGIO PUPINI, called DALLE LAME**
Recorded in Bologna 1511-1575

A GROUP OF MALE NUDES.

Pen and brown ink and wash over black chalk heightened with white, on grey paper. Squared in red chalk.
293 by 366mm.

Provenance: Richard Houlditch (L.2214); J. O'Connell; anonymous sale, London, Christie's, 11 April 1978, lot 17; anonymous sale, New York, Sotheby's, 18 January 1984, lot 100.

The subject of this drawing is unclear. It could conceivably be for a *Pentecost,* and Malvasia records a painting by Pupini of that subject in S. Petronio (see Malvasia, 1969, p.238/18).Malvasia also records a fresco by Pupini in the library of S. Salvatore, Bologna showing *St. Augustine Disputing with the Manicheans.* Unfortunately the fresco no longer exists, but Ugo Ruggeri has suggested that a drawing in Stockholm is of a preliminary study for that composition (see U. Ruggeri, 'Disegni di Oxford', *Critica d'Arte,* 154-156, 1977, p.100, illus. p.102, fig.3). It is tempting to suppose that the present group of figures might be related to the same fresco. It is unusual among Pupini's surviving drawings in being taken from posed studio models.

On the back of the mount is the following inscription, apparently in Mr. O'Connell's hand: *Hudson's mark is stamped on this drawing, although the name 'Pordenone' looks like Richardson's writing but whoever wrote it committed an error, as there is nothing of a Venetian character in the work, which evidently belongs to the School of Raphael, - and apparently the production of G.F. Penni called 'Il Fattore' a favorite pupil of Raphael. Vasari speaks of Penni being chiefly employed by Raphael on the cartoons - and it is remarkable that the two heads on the top to the right of the drawing are nearly identical in features to the heads of the first and third standing figures in the Cartoon of Christ's charge to Peter. The larger of these two heads in the drawing bears also a strong likeness to Penni's own face as seen in the Raphael drawing of it formerly in the Lawrence collection - Its highly finished execution agrees with Vasari's account of those he possessed by the Master. Can the subject be intended for the Delivery of the Souls from Limbo -the topmost figure pointing to the approaching Redeemer? The central figures are evidently intended for Adam and Eve - The upper head to the left shows where Parmigiano obtained his gracefully expressive heads. J. O'Connell.*

Private Collection, Paris

50 **LORENZO SABATINI, called LORENZINO DA BOLOGNA**
Bologna circa 1530 - Rome 1576

A SEATED ALLEGORICAL FIGURE OF JUSTICE, SEEN FROM BELOW.

Pen and brown ink and wash heightened with white, on blue paper. Octagonal.
194 by 203mm.

Provenance: G. and A. Neerman (as Palma Giovane), 1967; Timothy Clifford.

Literature: C. Johnston, *Mostra di disegni bolognesi dal xvi al xviii secolo,* Florence 1973, p.24, under cat. no.8; M. di Giampaolo, *Disegni Emiliani del Rinascimento,* Modena 1989, p.234.

In his life of Primaticcio, Vasari describes Lorenzo Sabatini as *pittore eccellente,* and responsible for the frescoes of six figures in the *ricetto* between the *Sala dei Cinquecento* and the *Sala dei Dugento* (see Vasari, *Le Vite,* Milanesi ed., vol.vii, p.415). The decoration of this antechamber was part of the project for the embellishment of the Palazzo Vecchio on the occasion of the wedding of Francesco de'Medici and Giovanna d'Austria in 1565. The present drawing is a study for the figure of Justice which appears on the vaulted ceiling of the room, balanced by the figure of Prudence, each in an octagonal frame decorated with grotesques. E. Allegri and A. Cecchi (in their *Guida storica: Palazzo Vecchio e i Medici,* Florence 1980, pp.284-85) mention two drawings related to the figure of Prudence. One, which seems to be a copy, is in the Staatliche Graphische Sammlung, Munich (inv. no.34851); the other is in the Uffizi (inv. no.15388F) and is, according to C. Johnston (*op.cit.),* in poor condition but autograph. Sabatini's preparatory drawing for another part of the ceiling, *Putti Holding Medici Emblems,* is also in the Uffizi (inv. no.12162F, Johnston, *op.cit.,* no.8).

Private Collection

51 LORENZO SABATINI, called LORENZINO DA BOLOGNA
Bologna circa 1530 - Rome 1576

ST. JEROME AND ST. GREGORY.

Pen and brown ink and reddish-brown wash heightened with white. Squared in red chalk.
288 by 188mm.

Provenance: William, 2nd Duke of Devonshire (L.718).

Literature: J. Winkelmann, 'Un frammento d'affresco di Lorenzo Sabatini', in *Studia Albornotiana,* Saragozza 1979, p.207, under note 13; M. di Giampaolo and S. Béguin, *Maestri Emiliani del Secondo Cinquecento,* Florence 1979, p.51, under no.38; M. Cazort and C. Johnston, *Bolognese Drawings in North American Collections, 1500-1800,* Ottawa 1982, p.53; J. Winkelmann, 'Lorenzo Sabatini detto Lorenzino da Bologna' in Fortunati, 1986, vol.ii, p.603, illus. p.625.

This is a preparatory study for one of Sabatini's two frescoes representing the Doctors of the Church, on the side walls of the Malvasia chapel in S. Giacomo, Bologna (fig.11). The decoration of the chapel, which is described by Malvasia (1969, p.84/20-26),also includes medallions of the four evangelists on the ceiling, and an altarpiece by Sabatini and Calvaert. Winkelmann dates the frescoes between 1566 and 1568. The chapel is considered Sabatini's major Bolognese commission after his return from Florence (see cat. no.50). The only other known drawing connected with the project is a study for the medallion of St. John the Evangelist, recently identified by Mario di Giampaolo in a private collection (see Winkelmann, *op.cit.,* 1986, p.603, illus. p.625).

The Duke of Devonshire and the Chatsworth Settlement Trustees

52 ORAZIO SAMACCHINI
Bologna 1532 - Bologna 1577

PROMETHEUS.

Bears an old attribution: *Masolino n.42.* Pen and brown ink and wash over black chalk. Squared in black chalk. Corners cut.
369 by 194mm.

Provenance: Herbert List (bears his dry stamp).

This cannot be connected with any known work by Samacchini, but the penwork and the definition of volumes are characteristic of his style. It is interesting to note the similarity of the figure of Prometheus to the Michelangelesque figure of Aeneas in a drawing by Daniele da Volterra in the Albertina (inv. no.497, see A. Perrig, *Michelangelo's Drawings,* New Haven 1991, pl.122). It may, therefore, be a work done while Samacchini was in Rome, working in the Sala Regia in the Vatican (1563/64).

Prometheus made a clay statue of a man in the image of a god and then, with the help of Minerva, stole fire from the gods and, by applying a torch to his statue, brought it to life. He was punished by Jupiter who had him chained to a rock and sent an eagle to eat his liver daily.

Private Collection

53 **ORAZIO SAMACCHINI**
Bologna 1532 - Bologna 1577

SUSANNAH BATHING.

Black chalk heightened with white. Made up at the top edge and bottom corners.
256 by 195mm.

Provenance: Anonymous sale, New York, Christie's, 10 January 1990, lot 42.

Julien Stock recognized this as the work of Samacchini when it was in the collection of the previous owner. It and the following drawing, *Joseph and Potiphar's Wife,* which are reunited here for the first time, are the preparatory studies for a pair of small panel paintings in the Uffizi (figs.24 and 23). In the old inventories the paintings were variously listed as by Bronzino, Allori and then Gregorio Pagani. Their attribution to Samacchini was first proposed by Philip Pouncey and accepted by Mina Gregori (*Gli Uffizi, Catalogo Generale,* Florence 1979, p.470). She dated the paintings around 1570, but Winkelmann disagrees and suggests 1565/66 (see J. Winkelmann in Fortunati, 1986, pp.636-37). Both this study and the one from Christ Church are characterized by a *sfumato* use of black chalk and white heightening which creates a particularly atmospheric effect. They reflect Samacchini's interest in Roman and Tuscan Mannerism, but in the less static execution and in the number of *pentimenti* they show an eclectic and less predictable side of his artistic personality.

Private Collection

54 **ORAZIO SAMACCHINI**
Bologna 1532 - Bologna 1577

JOSEPH AND POTIPHAR'S WIFE.

Bears numbers: *82* and *23.* Black chalk and stumping heightened with white chalk. Squared in black chalk.
327 by 277mm.

Provenance: General J. Guise.

Literature: J. Byam Shaw, *Drawings by Old Masters at Christ Church, Oxford,* Oxford 1976, vol.i, p.240, no.905, vol.ii, pl.545; M. Gregori, *Gli Uffizi, Catalogo Generale,* Florence 1979, p.470, under P1413.

See cat. no.53. As Mr. Byam Shaw notes, it was Philip Pouncey who identified this drawing as a preparatory study for the panel in the Uffizi (fig.23).

The Governing Body, Christ Church, Oxford (JBS 905)

82
23

55 **ORAZIO SAMACCHINI**
Bologna 1532 - Bologna 1577

STUDY FOR THE FIGURE OF CHRIST.

Black chalk. Squared in black chalk.
370 by 254mm.

Provenance: Sir Joshua Reynolds (L.2364); William Bates (L.2604); Lorna Lowe; anonymous sale, London, Christie's, 11 April 1978, lot 33; anonymous sale, London, Sotheby's, 18 November 1982, lot 20.

Literature: J. Winkelmann, 'Orazio Samacchini', in Fortunati, 1986, p.640, illus. p.668.

This is a preparatory study for the figure of Christ in Samacchini's altarpiece representing the Trinity, painted for the church of that name in Bologna (fig.19). The altarpiece is mentioned and praised by Malvasia (1969, p.261/25-30). The church has been suppressed, but the painting was recently rediscovered by Daniele Benati in the Olivetan convent of Santo Stefano. An engraving by Domenico Tibaldi of the composition is dated 1570 (see Bartsch, xviii, p.7, no.2), which leads Winkelmann to date the altarpiece around 1568/69 (Winkelmann, *op.cit.*, p.640). Another study for the figure of Christ, less finished and with variations in the drapery, is in the Uffizi (see C. Johnston, *Mostra di disegni bolognesi dal xvi al xviii secolo,* Florence 1973, p.24, no.9, fig.3). Other drawings for the commission are known: one of the whole composition in the Louvre (inv. no.2796), attributed by Philip Pouncey, and another in the Victoria and Albert Museum, *Putti holding a Globe* (see P. Ward-Jackson, *Italian Drawings,* London 1969, vol.i, no.310, illus.). It is interesting to note in the present drawing the striking similarity of the handling of the drapery to the style of Calvaert.

Private Collection

56 **ORAZIO SAMACCHINI**
Bologna 1532 - Bologna 1577

AN ANGEL.

Pen and brown ink and wash over black chalk heightened with white on blue paper. On the *verso* is an architectural design in pen and brown ink over black chalk.
230 by 130mm.

Provenance: Sir Peter Lely (L.2092); Thomas Hudson (L.2432); Shickman Gallery, New York; Christian Humann, his sale, New York, Sotheby's, 30 April 1982, lot 6 (as Lorenzo Sabatini).

As even Malvasia recognized, the works of Samacchini and Sabatini are frequently hard to distinguish. The present study cannot be connected with a known work by either artist, but an attribution to Samacchini seems more convincing than the previous one to Sabatini, on the basis of comparison with such secure Samacchini drawings as the very fine study for part of his decoration of the vault in the Duomo, Parma (1570), now in the Metropolitan Museum (see J. Bean and L. Turcić, *15th and 16th Century Italian Drawings in the Metropolitan Museum of Art,* New York 1982, no.235).

Private Collection

57 **ORAZIO SAMACCHINI**
Bologna 1532 - Bologna 1577

THE FLIGHT OF DAEDALUS AND ICARUS.

Bears number: *55*. Black chalk heightened with white, on blue paper. Partially squared in black chalk.
220 by 390mm.

Provenance: Jonathan Richardson, Snr. (L.2183); Charles Rogers (L.624); V. Ezekiel.

Exhibited: London, P.&D. Colnaghi, *Exhibition of Old Master Drawings,* 10 May-14 June 1956, no.15 (as Francesco Salviati).

Literature: A.W.A. Boschloo, *Il Fregio Dipinto a Bologna da Nicolò dell'Abate ai Carracci,* Bologna 1984, p.78; J. Winkelmann, 'Orazio Samacchini', in Fortunati, 1986, vol.ii, p.643.

Philip Pouncey first thought this drawing might be by Camillo Procaccini, whose graphic style it resembles. In 1968 he identified it as Samacchini's preparatory study for the fresco painted on a ceiling in the Palazzo Vizzani, Bologna *circa* 1575 (fig.28; see Malvasia, 1969, p.286/8-9). While the highly finished figure of Daedalus is very close to that in the fresco, the figure of Icarus is completely different, as are the indications of the signs of the zodiac.

Private Collection, Geneva

58 **PELLEGRINO TIBALDI**
Puria di Valsolda 1527 - Milan 1596

THE HOLY FAMILY WITH THE INFANT ST. JOHN THE BAPTIST.

Inscribed twice on the mount in brown ink: *Domenichino (from Benjamin West's collection previously in Jonathan Richardson's).* Pen and brown ink and wash over traces of black chalk heightened with white. Squared in black chalk.
416 by 253mm.

Provenance: Jonathan Richardson, Jnr. (L.2170); Benjamin West (L.419); anonymous sale, London, Sotheby's, 21 November 1974, lot 6.

Exhibited: Munich, Staatliche Graphische Sammlung, and elsewhere, *Stiftung Ratjen. Italienische Zeichnungen des 16.-18. Jahrhunderts,* 1977/78, p.146, cat. no.67.

Literature: J. Winkelmann, 'Pellegrino Tibaldi', in Fortunati, 1986, vol.ii, p.477, illus. p.497.

This impressive sheet was first attributed to Tibaldi by Philip Pouncey when it was sold in 1974. Although no painting of the composition is known, the high degree of finish and the squaring suggest that it must have been meant as a *modello.* It has generally been dated to Tibaldi's early years in Rome, *circa* 1548, and it already shows the hand of an accomplished artist in the well-balanced composition and in the monumental definition of the volumes. Jürgen Winkelmann sees in the composition a strong link to the classicizing tradition of Bolognese artists such as Innocenzo da Imola, and Bartolomeo and Giovambattista Bagnacavallo junior, and he particularly notes the similarity between the figure of the young Baptist in Tibaldi's drawing and the one in Bagnacavallo's *Sacra Conversazione* (illus. Winkelmann, *op.cit.,* p.438). Stylistically this drawing also resembles the *Tobias and the Angel* in the Uffizi (inv. no.477 Sant.) which was attributed to Tibaldi by John Gere (see J. Gere, 'Two late fresco cycles by Perino del Vaga: the Massimi Chapel and the Sala Paolina', in *The Burlington Magazine,* Jan. 1960, vol.cii, p.16, fig.23).

Stiftung Ratjen, Vaduz

59 **PELLEGRINO TIBALDI**
Puria di Valsolda 1527 - Milan 1596

POLYPHEMUS.

Bears old attribution: *Daniele da Volterra* and numbering: *37* and *20:B?*.
Black chalk.
517 by 384mm.

This hitherto unknown drawing, discovered by Julien Stock in 1990, relates to the figure of Polyphemus in one of the most spectacular and imaginative of Tibaldi's frescoes on the vaulted ceiling of the *Sala d'Ulisse* in the Palazzo Poggi (see fig.20). There are only a few differences between the drawing and the fresco: a slight variation in the position of the head and in the shape of the stone held in his right hand, as well as in the impression that the upper part of the body is pushed slightly foward. Light and shadow fall in a similar way in both the drawing and the fresco, creating an elaborate definition of volumes. Another black chalk study for the same figure is in the Kunsthalle, Hamburg (inv. no.21297). Although the head and the right arm are unfinished, the drawing is characterized by a skilful use of chalk and a very subtle definition of volumes. In comparison, the present study looks slightly drier in execution. The dating of Tibaldi's frescoes in the Palazzo Poggi has been extensively debated, but most critics now place them in the early 1550s, just after his return from Rome. They have strong stylistic connections with his Roman works and reflect the influence of Michelangelo and Daniele da Volterra, influences which are clear not only in the paintings but also in the technique of drawings such as the *Polyphemus*. Another fine example of Tibaldi's careful drawing style is the red chalk *Nude,* a study for one of the *ignudi* in the Palazzo Poggi (Copenhagen, Statens Museum for Kunst, illus. Winkelmann, in Fortunati, 1986, p.521).

Private Collection

Daniel da Volterra

60 **PELLEGRINO TIBALDI**
Puria in Valsolda 1527 - Milan 1596

THE ANNOUNCEMENT OF THE CONCEPTION OF ST. JOHN THE BAPTIST.

Pen and brown ink and wash over red chalk heightened with white. Arched top.
423 by 286mm.

Exhibited: London, Queen's Gallery, *Drawings by Michelangelo, Raphael, Leonardo and their Contemporaries,* 1972/73, no.135; Washington, National Gallery of Art and Parma, Galleria Nazionale, *Correggio and his Legacy,* 1984, no.104.

Literature: H. Bodmer, in Thieme-Becker, Leipzig 1939, vol.xxxiii, p.129; A.E. Popham and J. Wilde, *The Italian Drawings of the XV and XVI Centuries .... at Windsor Castle,* London 1949, no.947, fig.109; E. Feinblatt, 'A Drawing by Pellegrino Tibaldi', *Los Angeles County Museum Bulletin,* xiii, 2, 1961, p.12; S. Zamboni, 'La Cappella Poggi', in C. Volpe, *Il Tempio di S. Giacomo Maggiore,* Bologna 1967, p.153, fig.xlvi; M. Cazort and C. Johnston, *Bolognese Drawings in North American Collections,* Ottawa 1982, p.49, under cat. no.9; J. Bean and L. Turcić, *15th and 16th Century Italian Drawings in the Metropolitan Museum of Art,* New York 1982, p.241, under no.246; J. Winkelmann in Fortunati, 1986, vol.ii, pp.486-487, illus. p.527; R. Roli, 'Due disegni di Pellegrino Tibaldi', *Paragone,* 443, Florence 1987, p.36.

As Bodmer recognized, this sensational drawing is a preparatory study, with differences, for Tibaldi's fresco on the right wall of the Poggi Chapel in S. Giacomo Maggiore, Bologna (fig.22) which was one of the two major Bolognese commissions which Tibaldi received from Cardinal Giovanni Poggi (see cat. no.59). As with so much of Tibaldi's work, few documents survive by which to date the frescoes. Vasari mentions the Chapel after the decorations of the Palazzo Poggi, but this cannot be used as reliable chronological evidence (see Vasari, *Le Vite,* Milanesi ed., vol.vii, p.417). P. Lamo, a contemporary source, writes in his *Graticola di Bologna* that the chapel was completed in 1560 except for the altarpiece. Modern scholars have continued to debate the chronology of the execution of the two Poggi commissions: Winkelmann (*op.cit.*) and Diane De Grazia (Washington/Parma exhib. cat., *op.cit.*) give summaries of the various opinions. Cardinal Poggi died in 1556 and was buried in the chapel. The altarpiece was completed by Prospero Fontana in 1561. Two other drawings related to the same fresco are known: a red chalk study for the figure of St. Elizabeth is in the Musée Atger, Montpellier and another highly finished study, also in red chalk, for the same figure with a servant behind is in a private collection (R. Roli, *op.cit.*). A drawing for the lower half of the other fresco in the chapel, *St. John Baptizing the Multitude,* is in the Metropolitan Museum of Art, New York.

(continued)

(continued)
The representation of the subject (Luke I, 5-25) is most unusual iconographically, but characteristic of Tibaldi's unconventional approach. The drawing, so different from the careful chalk manner of the Polyphemus (cat. no.59), shows another aspect of his style. As Diane De Grazia writes: 'His pen and ink and wash drawings, often heightened with white, can be fantastical in conception and show a dependence on Perino in the decorative pen work, but are uniquely his own in the exaggeration of features' (Washington/Parma, *op.cit.*, p.331).

Lent by Her Majesty the Queen

61 **BOLOGNESE SCHOOL, 16TH CENTURY**

STUDIES OF THE HOLY FAMILY.

Bears monogram: *LCfe.* and on the back of the mount old attributions to Lodovico Carracci. Pen and brown ink and wash heightened with white, on coarse buff paper.
175 by 240mm.

Provenance:
Dr. G. Laporte (L.1170); anonymous sale, London, Sotheby's, 30 June 1986, lot 155 (as Giacomo Cavedone).

This drawing has traditionally been associated with Bologna. The suggestion that it might be by Cavedone was rejected by Laura Giles. The facial types and the exaggeration of the hands have more in common with the work of Tibaldi, so an attribution to him or to one of his circle seems more convincing.

Private Collection

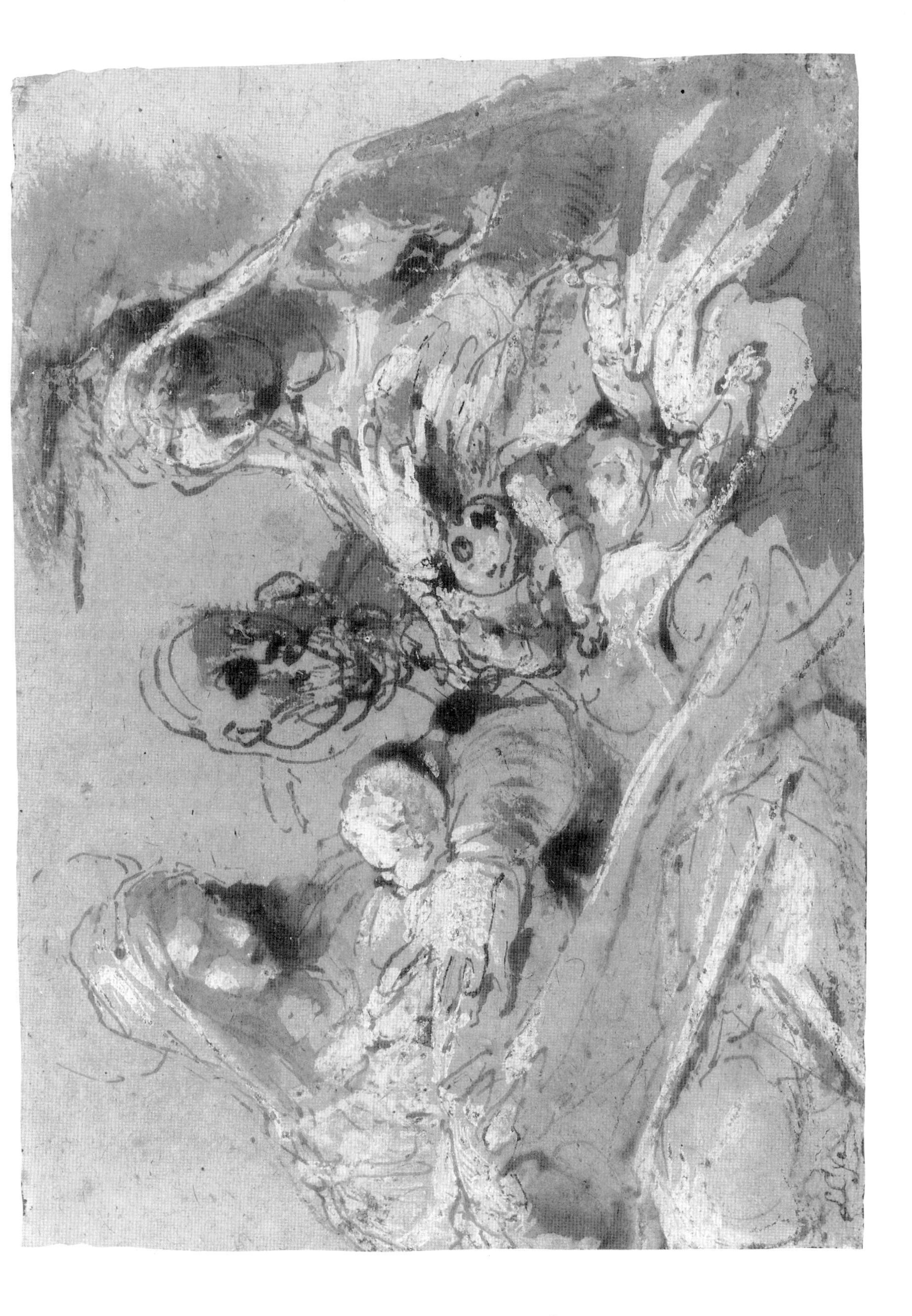

Fig.1. Cesi: *The Adoration of the Magi.* Pinacoteca Nazionale, Gabinetto dei Disegni.

Fig.2. Cesi: *A Carthusian Saint.* S. Gerolamo alla Certosa, Bologna.

Fig.3. Cesi: *An Allegory of Fidelity and Silence.* Palazzo Magnani, Bologna.

Fig.4. Cesi: *The Adoration of the Magi.* S. Domenico, Bologna.

Fig.5. Faccini: *Studies of Heads. Verso* cat. no.25.

Fig.6. Faccini: *Figures studies. Verso* cat. no.27.

Fig.7. Nosadella: *The Annunciation.* Art Museum, Princeton University.

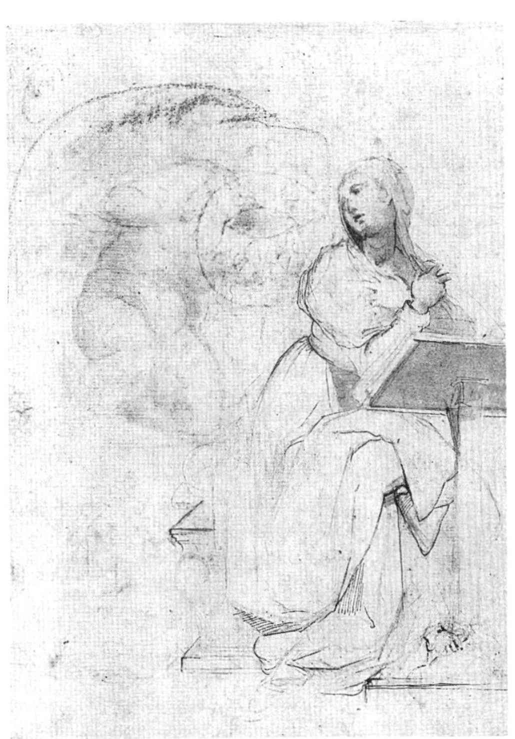

Fig.8. Nosadella: *The Annunciation. Verso* cat. no.37.

Fig.9. Passserotti: *The Madonna in Glory with St. Petronius, St. Dominic and the Martyrdom of St. Peter Martyr.* S. Petronio, Bologna.

Fig.10. Passerotti: *The Adoration of the Magi.* Palazzo Arcivescovile, Bologna.

Fig.11. Sabatini: *St. Jerome and St. Gregory.* S. Giacomo Maggiore.

Fig.12. Annibale Carracci: *The Assumption.* Gemäldegalerie Dresden.

Fig.13. After Calvaert, by Thomassin: *The Marriage at Cana.*

Fig.14. Calvaert: *The Lamentation.* Galleria Nazionale, Parma.

Fig.15. Calvaert: *St. Gregory and the Miracle of the Brandeum.* S. Gregorio, Bologna.

Fig.16. Cavazzoni: *St. Catherine before Maxentius.* Castel S. Pietro, Bologna.

Fig.17. Innocenzo da Imola: *The Madonna and the Child with Saint.* S. Giacomo Maggiore, Bologna.

Fig.18. Lavinia Fontana: *The Crucifixion with St. Jerome and Two Patrons.* Palazzo Pepoli, Bologna.

Fig.19. Samacchini: *The Trinity.* S. Stefano, Bologna.

Fig.20. Tibaldi: *Polyphemus.* Palazzo Poggi, Bologna.

Fig.21. Girolamo da Treviso: *Madonna and Child in Glory with St. Jerome and St. Catherine of Alexandria.* Narodowe Muzeum, Warsaw.

Fig.22. Tibaldi: *The Announcement of the Conception of St. John the Baptist.* S. Giacomo Maggiore.

Fig.23. Samacchini: *Joseph and Putiphar's wife.* Uffizi, Florence.

Fig.24. Samacchini: *Susannah Bathing.* Uffizi, Florence.

Fig.25. Agostino Carracci: *Cephalus and Aurora.* Palazzo Farnese, Rome.

Fig.26. Lodovico Carracci: *The Flagellation.* Musée de la Chartreuse, Douai.

Fig.27. Nicolò dell' Abate: *Hercules Killing the Nemaean Lion.* Palazzo Poggi, Bologna.

Fig.28. Samacchini: *The Flight of Daedalus and Icarus.* Palazzo Vizzani, Bologna.

Photographic Sources

Windsor Castle, Royal Library, Her Majesty the Queen

Courtauld Institute of Art

The Governing Body, Christ Church, Oxford

Photography: Deborah Phillips

Printed in Great Britain by Saunders & Williams (Printers) Ltd, Belmont, Sutton, Surrey

NOTES